HAVERIM

The Four Lost Levels of Study

paulclayton**gibbs**

part one of the ancient trilogy

Haverim: The Four Lost Levels of Study
Copyright © 2013 by Paul Clayton Gibbs

Published by Harris House Publishing
www.harrishousepublishing.com
Arlington, Texas
USA

This title is also available in other formats.

Cover creation by Lauren Hill; design by Paul Clayton Gibbs
Cover background image ©angelp / Crestock
Author's photo by Paul Green
Production team: Terry Tamashiro Harris | Sebrina Miller | Lauren Hill | Rebecca Royal

Library of Congress Cataloging-in-Publication Data

Gibbs, Paul Clayton, 1964 -
    Haverim: The Four Lost Levels of Study / Paul Clayton Gibbs
        p.cm
    Includes biographical references
    ISBN 978-0-9824160-6-8•(pbk.)
    1. Bible—Study and teaching. 2. Christianity and Culture. I. Title.
BS600.3.G53   2013

                       2013935797

Printed in the United States of America.

This book is dedicated to

*Harry Letson for passing on your desire to study
and the courage to look at different angles*

*Henny Letson for the constant
encouragement every time I taught*

*Paul & Paula, John & Karen, Ian & Jan
for making it about Jesus and not religion*

Contents

IMAGINE

Why?

Co-op

I once decided to read through the Bible in a year.

So, while working as a young manager in a department store, I spent every lunch hour, as well as the shorter morning and afternoon tea breaks, in a small room at the back of the building. While everyone else was in the canteen, I pored over my Bible and study aid, determined to reach my goal within twelve months. And, as an added bonus to my spiritual development, every Friday I fasted.

I grew in my knowledge of the chronological order of the Bible: its people, places, events, and teachings. And now, as I look over my life, I realize . . .

It was one of the most *idiotic* things I ever did.

I spent an entire year, avoiding my workmates in the cafeteria, to study about God's heart for my workmates in the cafeteria.

It takes practice to be that foolish.

God has put brains in our heads, conscience in our hearts, and His Spirit in our lives. So how did I become so habitually dull-witted? Why did it take my colleagues challenging me about my lack of friendship to snap me out of it?

Was it because church culture taught me to learn the things of God without giving me an equal understanding of how to share them? And, if so . . . why?

Pull

It has been said that:

> Our *methods* must change, but our *message* must stay the same.

I like this. It feels right. It seems correct.

Unfortunately, it is not.

You see, our *methods* have never changed until our *message* has changed first.

I have been a Christian for over thirty years and, even in that short time, I have seen how fresh understanding of Jesus' invitation has shaped the way we do things. When our message was simply *'turn or burn,'* our methods were limited to *'smash and grab'* evangelism with the goal of getting people to say a prayer and then placing them in a church that could keep them spiritually safe.

For many years, we have been taught the Bible a certain way. The problem is that the world is changing, but our practices have remained unchallenged.

It has also been said that:

> "If you want something you've never had before, you must be willing to *do* something you've never done before."[1]

Again, although true, this is also a little shortsighted because in reality:

> If you want to do something you've never done before, you will have to *believe* something you've never believed before.

Some of us have been Christians for a long time, but rather than going on exciting new journeys, we seem to be stuck in a scene from Scooby-Doo. We may appear to move forward, but we keep seeing the same predictable scenery repeating itself in the background.[2]

We may believe God can do something fresh, but some of us rarely see anything but stale results. We struggle with the same old struggles because we connect with Him in the same old ways.

So what needs to change about our beliefs when it comes to the study of the Bible?

My friend Matt works at an advertising agency. He often helps me think through our use of social media to promote the mission of the Pais Movement. We share resources; I have taught at his workplace as a consultant, and he has spoken at various Pais conferences. According to Matt, the advertising industry has had to take a new perspective in its response to a fundamental shift within society in the last three to four years. In the past, agencies like his determined what the customer heard and saw. More recently, however, through the internet and other interactive technology, the customers dictate their own schedules.

Information, learning, and understanding face a new methodology.

From *push* to *pull*.

In the past, advertisements were *pushed* onto potential customers, but now those same people only *pull* the information they want to see.

Have you noticed that the way you want to learn is changing? I see it in my two boys. According to *The New York Times*, they are the first generation for years to actually watch *less* television than their elders.[3] Instead of being presented with a pre-determined menu of limited options, they hit the internet like ravenous wolves seeking out the things that interest them. They have become expert researchers. Many believe that something has changed regarding how we are now shaped to receive information. However, I wonder . . .

Has it really changed or was understanding always best grasped in a different way?

Is it true that we find the Bible difficult to understand *or* is it truer that the difficulty in understanding stems from the way we attempt to teach it?

Does the Bible have a middle-management problem?

Maybe we need to rediscover an *ancient* method for our *post-modern* times.

Epic

I have been on a journey, a search to find a way not only to study the Bible ourselves, but to help our colleagues at work, our fellow students, and the people in our communities find the Kingdom of God—a way forward that is easily transferable and does not need a Ph.D., a brain the size of China, or a particularly religious setting. I have been driven to rediscover what Jesus had in mind when His Spirit prompted the writer of Hebrews to challenge:

> *In fact, though by this time you ought to be teachers, you need some- one to teach you the elementary truths of God's word all over again. You need milk, not solid food!* [4]

Then one day, my worlds collided: the world of the millennials I lead and that of the ancient rabbis I studied.

Suddenly, something clicked. I realized that my very question— how to communicate with and train those who reject the modern era's packaging of simplistic 'cause and effect' solutions—was leading me to the lost arts of Jesus' contemporaries.

It turned out that Jesus had all the answers!

Actually, that's not quite right either. It turned out that He had all the *questions*.

I had discovered that most books on post-modernity were not really about post-modernity at all, but were just commentaries on the modern world and how it was changing. One book, however, pointed out that even though we don't really know what this new age will fully look like, we can recognize some of its emerging values. [5]

The author uses the acronym of E.P.I.C. to explain them. I have made some slight alterations and included my own interpretation to help us see the opportunities.

Experiential: In the modern world, instructions were given to be *executed*; in this emerging world, invitations are offered to be *experienced*.

Participatory: In the modern world, opportunities were presented to be *performed*; in this emerging world, people are encouraged to *participate*.

Imaginative: In the modern world, images were used to *present answers*; in this emerging world, images are required to *provoke questions*.

Connected: In the modern world, *consumption* drove individualism; in this emerging world, *connectivity* recreates consumerism.

As you ponder these simple values, perhaps you can relate to them. I know I can. I also see how Jesus' methods of grasping truth and passing it on mesh so very well with them.

I feel hope.

I am encouraged.

I imagine a way forward.

Velocity

The world is not changing; the world *has* changed.

At the end of the last century, in his book *Business @ the Speed of Thought*, Bill Gates declared that for successful business in the eighties, the key word had been 'quality,' in the nineties it was 'innovation,' and he prophesied that in the noughties, it would be 'velocity.'[6]

He suggested that the companies that would do best in the new century would be those who could respond most quickly to the changing needs of its clients. I remember thinking to myself at the time how sad it is that the world responds so speedily to the 'holy customer' and yet the Church responds so slowly to the Holy Spirit.

The world has changed . . . It is *reverting*.

The ways in which Jesus understood and unpacked the scriptures are in vogue. More than that, they are essential. To comprehend the Bible in a way that will open up a whole new world for us, we must grasp hold of what Jesus understood it to be. Then, we can let His *message* contained within it shape our *methods* for teaching it. To do this, He wishes to lead us through *experience*, giving us a method where we can *participate* in the study of God's dream. He wants to pose questions in our *imagination* in order that we can *connect* with one another as together we discover how His dream of Heaven coming to Earth can happen.

Or as the ancient Hebrews once referred to it . . . *Haverim*.

What?

Dim

Why are many post-modern churches producing pre-reformation Christians?

Before the reformation, when the only organized and recognized church was the Catholic Church of Rome, it refused to allow scripture to be available in any language other than Latin. The people of God had to completely rely on those few religious professionals who could pass on the Bible's message. They could not unravel it for themselves. No one could question an interpretation because few people, other than priests, could read it. For the most part in today's evangelical churches, the Bible may as well be written only in Latin once again.

Few study it.

Even less pass it on.

We get all of our interpretation from the leaders we idolize. We are more likely to know the words of Max, Bill, Rick, and Francis than we are to know the words of Matthew, Mark, Luke, and John.[7]

We may not live in the *dark* ages anymore, but when it comes to understanding the Word of God, we live in the days of willing ignorance, the era of acceptable limitations.

We live in the *'dim* ages.'

Culture

We need, therefore, to go beyond *curriculum* to *culture*.

If we truly believe that God will change our world and use our churches to do it, then now is the time to build our great, attractive, relevant churches with His understanding of study in mind.

The inventor Sir James Dyson said that reinvention requires a passionate anger about something that doesn't work.[8]

And something isn't working, is it?

By that, I mean the purely invitational approach that brings in a crowd through a great presentation to 'study the Bible' by filling in blanks on a worksheet. *That* idea is compromised, incomplete, and a little perverted.[9]

It can grow *churches*, but does it grow His *Kingdom*?

In most churches, only core members attend Bible studies, and they rarely experience a method of study that can be easily reproduced in other settings or for other passages and topics.

A Bible class experience teaches them *what* to think, not *how* to think.

I am committed to getting people on the same page and drawing them to absolute truth. The problem with most curricula, however, is that they ultimately teach us to search for answers, but not for God. And by answers, I mean the *one* answer of the *one* presenter. Once we know that one answer, we quickly get bored. The Word of God becomes cliché: something profound, but weakened by constant repetition of the same over-used explanations.

It loses its vitality. It loses its surprise.

The further problem is that this method of study does not equip us to share that truth with others. It is inflexible, uncreative, and outdated. We live in a new world, with new opportunities, and the need for a new transferable way to share our Gospel.

As I write this chapter, I am sitting at a table in my local Starbucks. Nearby sits an older gentleman who is smartly dressed and a touch debonair. He has just tucked a paper napkin into his collar as he tries to avoid dripping mayonnaise while negotiating a turkey and cheese sandwich. I am wondering how I can start a conversation with him.

If I do manage to chat with him and he shows an interest in discovering faith in Jesus, I know that I now have a new way of sharing it with him—one that approaches the Bible from whatever angle *he* needs to approach it, one that will present questions not just answers, and one that will guide him through a multi-faceted journey until he can discover for himself the truth of Jesus.

I am also sitting here wondering how other followers of Jesus would feel in my position right now. Would they even want to start that conversation, or would they avoid it because they have no idea how to unpack the scriptures with a neighbor?

Is the spirit willing, but the training weak?

I think it may be.

Haverim

My mission is to make missionaries.

In the Pais Movement, we do this through *Haverim*: a culture of joining with others to approach the scriptures differently in order that you can be the Bible in your community.

Haver means 'friends,' and in Biblical times, the word *haverim* specified 'friends who studied together.' All over the world—in Europe, Africa, Asia, North America, and South America—through Pais, young people and adults are exploring this new, yet ancient method on a daily basis.

A key part of the Haverim process is the way in which we study together. We call it Haverim Devotions™ or HD for short. Yet Haverim is not primarily about providing another Bible study program in a church, but about sparking a culture where the saints are equipped to teach in their communities.

The Church again becomes a training center.

Not the place to simply come and learn, but the place to come and learn *how to teach*.

That is what this book is about; it aims to give you *inspiration* and *information*, trusting that you will take them both and influence your world.

Cloud

If you do want to influence your world, let me share a key way that this book can help you. I do want it to help, but it is not entirely up to me if it does. You will need to play your part, and the first step might be to ask yourself a particular question:

Why do you study the Bible?

An English politician, when asked to give a one-word summary of Christianity, replied:

"Choice." [10]

It was an unusual but insightful reply.

Following God is not about one big choice but several million little ones. The type of choice we think it is about is of paramount importance.

In my book about the Kingdom Principles, I share the motif of 'the cloud and the line,' the idea being that many of us live life as if on a line. [11] At one extreme are the things we *must not do* in order to avoid punishment and its consequences; at the opposite extreme are the things we feel we *must do* in order to gain any possible reward. 'Line-dwelling' is the term used for a faith that is based upon trying to work out where you should be on the line. We can get hypnotized by the line, spending our efforts fixating on the dos and don'ts in order to squeeze out a better life. We sow with the reaping in mind. We judge with our judgment in mind. We humble ourselves with our own exalting in mind.

We miss the *point* because we miss the *perspective*.

There is a cloud.

God's true heart and intention reside there. Clouds are mentioned often in the Bible as the presence of God appearing in a cloud.[12]

He seeks to be sought.

Christianity is a pursuit. It is seeking His heart on all matters so that we can make choices that please Him, and if these choices are to be well-informed, we need to hear what He is *really* trying to tell us. My goal is to help us read the Bible for a different purpose . . . to see the heart of God.

Haverim Devotions™ are split into four levels. Each one feels different from the other, but they all aim to take us much deeper, discovering meaning in God's words and our lives.

> The *intended* meaning
> The *implied* meaning
> The *interpreted* meaning
> The *inspired* meaning

Each level gives a fresh perspective, and this new perspective will produce new results.

Yet as you read on, you will be challenged at each level to decide which type of devotion to God and His Word you want to pursue:

> The *line* or the *cloud?*

How?

Pardes

The pursuit of the cloud started a long time ago, in a world distant, yet not so distinct, from ours.

During the middle ages, rabbis looked back on the time of Jesus and noticed various methods of both understanding and passing on the Word of God that were used in the second temple period.[13]

Some named this methodology *PaRDeS*.[14]

Pardes is a word with Persian origins and means 'orchard,' 'park,' or more specifically, a 'garden of knowledge.'

Later hijacked by mystics and Gnostics, some of its many benefits have been lost to us. In fact, although understanding *pardes* has helped shed light on the teaching of Jesus, I have not found a single Christian book written solely on the subject.

Did we throw out the baby with the bath water? Or, is it that we simply have thought so little of the importance of Jesus' culture that we never ran the bath in the first place?

Although the term *pardes* was unlikely to have existed in the time of Jesus, the word itself hints at His ancient and dynamic form of teaching. It reminds us that much of a rabbi's ministry occurred within the community, perhaps under a tree or atop a grassy hill, with eager students and disciples experiencing not just the words, but participating in the actions of their role model.

PaRDeS is where we derive the word 'paradise' from, and it is an acronym of four parts:

P'shat
R'mez
D'rash
S'od

I have taken these ancient ideas and transferred them into the world in which we live today. In doing so, I am finding them to be a phenomenal way to engage those looking to *experience, participate, imagine,* and *connect* in order to search for the heart of God. They also help those simply searching for a God to know.

I am presenting these ideas, not to tickle academic thinking, but to equip the saints for works of service. I have put practical applications to them and will share creative ideas to implement each part.

I have reshaped, rethought, reformatted, and retold them.

What I cannot do, however, is reengineer their dynamics.

You see, they still only work for those pursuing God, not the law; yet incredibly, they work for those inside as well as those still outside the Kingdom who are seeking.

So, let's start digging.

Garden

Many kings and queens have sought to bring their version of the perfect world to Earth. The largest empire in the world was of course the British Empire, which covered a third of the globe at its peak. As an Englishman, I am therefore very aware of the human desire to force its will—what may seem its good and pleasing will—upon those who have a different understanding.

It was one of our queens of whom it was said:

Mary, Mary, quite contrary, How does your garden grow?
With silver bells and cockleshells,
And pretty maids all in a row.

At first sight, this familiar English nursery rhyme flows from the lips and conjures up a pretty picture of flowers, jewels, and beautiful people. Beneath the surface, however, lies a different story.

A historical interpretation of this common rhyme tells us that the Mary alluded to was Mary Tudor, the daughter of King Henry the VIII, unaffectionately known as 'Bloody Mary.' She was a staunch Catholic remembered for forcing her religion through violence. The 'garden' mentioned represents the graveyards of her enemies, and the 'pretty maids' refer to the original instrument that could take up to eleven blows to sever a human head from its shoulders. History records that the inefficient maiden led to victims resisting and being chased around a scaffold; therefore, maidens were later replaced with the more 'humane' mechanical instrument known as 'the guillotine.' The 'silver bells' refer to thumb screws, an instrument of torture, and the 'cockleshells' speak of something unspeakable that was used on the male genitals.

This pretty little song is not what it first appears to be; it is a protest song! It was an indictment of not only the unpopular Mary, but also her way of spreading her kingdom. Mary advanced her empire with violence, fear, and power resulting from a heady blend of religion and politics that at many times could not be separated.

Jesus grows His Kingdom in a different way. His is also described in stories that involve gardens and things that are found in them. In fact, the Bible is really a story of three important trees: the tree of the knowledge of good and evil, the tree of Calvary, and the tree that starts the story and ends it—the tree of life in the book of Genesis and the tree of life in the book of Revelation.

A tree that starts in a garden, but ends up in a city.

God's garden is a garden that grows. Two thousand years ago, thirteen people were familiar with the Lord's Prayer, and yet on a recent Easter Sunday it was estimated that two billion Christians recited it across the world. So how can the paradise to which Jesus alluded touch our streets, flow through our offices, and permeate our schools?

It cannot be something we are *enforcing*. It must be something God is *endorsing*.

It cannot be *pushed*. It must be *pulled*.

It poses the question:

> Who has the ears to hear what is being said?

Hearers

Jesus tells the story of a farmer, a type of gardener, to explain what it takes for His Kingdom to flourish. The parable involves a man who sows seed. Some seed lands on a path, some on rocks, others on thorns, and the last seed falls on good soil.[15]

Now first of all, we have to ask ourselves, "What does the seed represent?"

It represents Jesus' message. His message was an invitation to join His mission of seeing the Kingdom come. It starts with repentance, but it doesn't end there. It does not end with a better spiritual life or religion. In fact, it does not really end anywhere. It is an invitation to get involved and keep getting involved in seeing His Kingdom come more and more in our own lives and in the lives of others.

The agricultural landing zones are metaphors for different attitudes. Let me invite you to consider *which* of the four soils best represents you.

The first soil is found along the path:

> "... *Some fell along the path, and the birds came and ate it up.*"

The path represents those who don't really accept their place in the Kingdom, and so their enemy gobbles up that dream before it can even find a place to root.

The little they rejected is snatched away.

The second soil is located among rocks:

> "Some fell on rocky places, where it did not have much soil. It sprang up quickly, because the soil was shallow. But when the sun came up, the plants were scorched, and they withered because they had no root."

The rocky area refers to those who receive the message of the Kingdom with joy. They are pleased to hear about God's plan. It speaks to them of a better life. They do not, however, really own that dream themselves. It does not root so deeply that it becomes something they want to see spread in others. In their minds, it was just meant for them. So, when persecution comes and when what they get is less than what they hoped for, it is easily uprooted.

The fire they had is burned away.

The third soil is found where thorns grow:

> "Other seed fell among thorns, which grew up and choked the plants."

The thorns tell us of those who are excited, enthused, and even idealistic. The message becomes their dream as well. Over time, however, other visions come in that take over. The more seductive dreams of stuff, status, and the thorns that make them prickly become their primary concern. The mission may remain; it is rarely discarded, but there is not enough space in their lives to let the seed grow beyond a weak and withered shoot.

The growth they had is stunted.

The fourth soil is good soil:

> "Still other seed fell on good soil, where it produced a crop—a hundred, sixty or thirty times what was sown."

The good soil represents those that hear the exact same message as the other three, yet the seeds sown in them grow and flourish. The fruit they produce is not because things are easier or their lives less full. What makes them fruitful is not belief, faith, or conviction. According to Jesus, what makes them good soil for the invitation of the Kingdom is a commodity rarely talked about—a commodity this book aims to give you.

The message they received is *expedited*.

But what is this rare commodity?

There are five thousand parables in Judaism. Jesus was not unusual for using them. In fact, many of His parables were twists on those that already existed. The four soils were in fact His contribution to an often-used rabbinic formula.

The *mishnah*,[16] meaning 'repetition,' employs it in the parable of the four kitchen utensils: the sponge, the funnel, the strainer, and the sift.[17] Gamaliel, a well respected Jewish teacher and contemporary of Jesus, spoke of the parable of four fish: the fish that is unclean, the fish that is clean, the fish from the Jordan River, and the fish from the Mediterranean.

Why were the parables of the four hearers so popular? Because they were the perfect formula to teach the commodity that leads to multiplication:

> *"But the seed falling on good soil refers to someone who hears the word and understands it. This is the one who produces a crop, yielding a hundred, sixty or thirty times what was sown."*[18]

Understanding.

Fable

As we begin to unpack this way of studying life, let's realize what it is for and what it is not for.

Haverim Devotions™ offer the opportunity to search for not only the heart of God, but for the mind of Christ. That journey, however, must be undertaken for all the right reasons.

A fable in Jewish folklore about the four levels of *Pardes* goes:

> "Four men entered paradise. One looked and died; one looked and
> went mad; one destroyed the plants; and one entered in peace and
> departed in peace."[19]

This is interpreted to mean that four men searched for the 'secret knowledge' of God. The first died a spiritual death and lost what he once had. The second went mad. The third committed heresy. Only the fourth left in peace.

How you enter the Word of God will often determine how you leave it. This Jewish folklore warns us of the age-old dangers of searching for God's secret wisdom.

It is not for *status*.

We should not seek understanding in order to prove ourselves better than others. One of the dangers in getting perhaps too engrossed in Judaism and its rituals is that we may fall afoul of the religious pride that seems to accompany it. Jesus taught us that true wisdom is seen in those who are truly humble.

It is not for *salvation*.

The mysteries of the mystical religions of Jesus' day were needed for redemption. These mystery religions were exclusive. Only certain people could ever know their secrets. They were esoteric in nature. Jesus stressed that salvation comes through Him and that *anyone* who seeks will find.

So, if it is not for status and it is not for salvation, what *is* it for?

It is for *establishing*.

Establishing on earth the Kingdom of Heaven. Establishing the Kingdom within your heart to such an extent that it overflows into your world.

Jesus is asking the question, *"Do you want to see what I see?"*

Scriptures

Haverim Devotions™ are simply a tool. They are the four levels used by friends who study together to find God in the Bible.

God is . . . The Father, The Son, and The Holy Spirit.

God is *not* . . . The Father, The Son, and The Holy Scriptures.

The four levels I am about to share with you are not an end to themselves. It must be understood therefore, that a Haverim group is the community that reaches out to its neighbors, and the Haverim Devotions™ study tool should not take up every week that the Haverim meets together.

HD is also not simply a study of the Bible; it is a study of life itself.

It can be used to help your friend at work or your neighbor understand bigger issues than simply religion. Hopefully as you share your faith in your world, some people will want to find out more. They may even come to you with specific issues that they want to discuss. Most of the time you will want to simply chat these through, but sometimes you may wish to offer them a chance to look into things a little more deeply. In that case, HD can help you. You can offer to take them through four ways to discover more using the Bible, or you can employ just one of the levels if you feel that is best.

If you are a follower of Jesus, can I encourage you to practice studying the Bible in this ancient way so that it becomes second nature to you? As it does, you will be able to spot where people are on their journey and you will be equipped to assist them.

Adopting Jesus' philosophy that we should teach those who want to be taught, this way of studying does require a person to lean forward—a person who is searching. They can be an agnostic, atheist, Muslim, Hindu, a non-practicing or disconnected Christian, but they must be wanting to hear from you.

Your job becomes one of a tour guide rather than a travel agent. You are not presenting somewhere you have never been yourself, but you are partnering with them in the journey, offering to facilitate their trip and pointing out things of interest along the way.

This is not a list of steps to execute, but an invitation to come and experience.

This is not a presentation tool, but a participation tool.

This is not a matter of providing the right answers, but rather provoking the right questions.

This is not an opportunity to consume knowledge, but to connect with others to share it.

People are different and Haverim Devotions™ take advantage of that. One of the levels is especially attractive to those who love *research*, one for those who enjoy *riddles*, one for those who find pleasure in *relationship*, and one for those who love *reflecting*.

Yet each level can help us understand something of the heart of God behind the story of God.

INTENDED

P'shat

Why?

Surface

Imagine that when the Word of God hits your heart it could go deeper than the surface.

> *". . . Some fell along the path, and the birds came and ate it up."* [20]

Ever felt that your understanding of God was superficial?

Ever felt that you've followed God for superficial reasons?

Maybe there is a connection.

God has planted hidden things. He has not hidden them *from* us but *for* us. He has hidden them for when we are ready to understand them. He has hidden things in nature, and the more we discover about our universe, the more we see signs and metaphors of God's plan and wisdom, His nature and super-nature. He has hidden things in humankind; the ways our bodies work are biological object lessons. The more we discover about the body, the more we learn about His plan for the body of Christ.

Consider this puzzle:

> I cdnuolt blveiee taht I cluod aulaclty uesdnatnrd waht I was raednig. The aamizng pweor of the hmuan mind! Aoccdrnig to rscheearch at Cmabrigde Uinervtisy, it deosn't mttaer in waht oredr the ltteers in a wrod are, the olny iprmoatnt tihng is taht the frist and lsat ltteer are

in the rghit pclae. The rset can be a tatol mses and you can sitll raed it wouthit a porbelm.

It is interesting to me that this ability was wired into our brains long before English was invented. It works for most western languages but not for others such as Hebrew. What is the implication here?

Well, please read these two sentences:

> A vheclie epxledod at a plocie cehckipont near the UN haduqertares in Bagahdd on Mnoday kilinlg the bmober and an Irqai polcie offceir.

And then read this:

> A pdietairc psyhiacin has aitmtded the magltheuansr of a tageene ceacnr pintaet who deid aetfr a hatospil durg blendur.

The same rules apply, but the second is usually much harder to read.

Why? Because we do not understand its *context*. We are unfamiliar with some of the medical terms, therefore we cannot feel the spirit in which it was written.

To enter the Kingdom come, we must see what at first cannot be seen. We need to feel what at first cannot be felt. We need to taste what at first cannot be tasted.

The first level of the Haverim Devotions™ will teach us how to do just that. It will help us find the *context* required to comprehend God's *point* . . . not because we cannot see His point, but because it may be so engulfed by our culture that we cannot see it clearly.

The rabbis taught in gardens. Sometimes they sat down to teach in synagogues or the portico of the temple, but more often they taught in vineyards, orchards, and parks. In doing so, they were able to help their disciples taste their *Torah*.[21] They could see the starkness of a withered fig tree; they could enjoy the beauty of a field of lilies. They could touch the good soil that crumbled in their fingers or feel the sun-scorched path beneath their feet. They could scratch their ankles on the wild thorns or twist them while walking on a rocky outcrop.

They were not just listening to their rabbi's teaching; they were *absorbing* it.

Yet some things were still hidden from them . . . things planted secretly under the soil. They could not feel, taste, smell, hear, or see those things.

That is, not until they dug for them.

Without understanding, we have less awareness of God's purpose for *why* we should do what we do. Without awareness, we lack intention, and without intention, what we do may not be as fruitful as we had hoped.

Just like the final puzzle, we struggle to put the pieces together.

What?

Context

The first level of Haverim Devotions™ is the *intended* meaning.

The *intended* meaning is the obvious, straightforward message of a passage.

The Hebrew word for this level is *p'shat* and means 'simple.'

The method of the *intended* meaning is to seek *context*.

The Bible comes to light when you can start to *feel* the setting in which it was happening. So we do this by engaging in a discovery of its history, culture, and timeline. Often we can misunderstand what Jesus was saying simply because we no longer understand *how* He was saying it, *when* He was saying it, and even *why* He was saying it.

If we miss His context, we miss His point.

At this level when we look at a passage, we ask questions such as:

> Who wrote it?
>
> Why did they write it?
>
> Where were they when they wrote it?
>
> What does history teach us about the people involved?
>
> What does archaeology reveal about the place involved?
>
> What might the manners and customs of the day tell us about what happened or what was being said?

Later we will look at how you can do this without having to be a historian, Bible scholar, or archaeologist, but first, let me give you two examples of what I have discovered at this level.

Seven

In one culture-shaping bit of history, the Bible records when Nicodemus, a member of the Sanhedrin, the council of religious lawmakers, approached Jesus. In this conversation, Jesus employed the famous 'born again' phrase. Many think that Jesus coined the idiom 'born again' and that the phrase itself is the key to what He was teaching Nicodemus.

But He did not and it was not.

The maxim 'born again' and its variations already existed in Jesus' day. In fact, six uses of it were well-known.[22] You were born again when:

1. *You got married.*

2. *You converted and were baptized into Judaism.*

3. *You became a son of the commandments.*

4. *You were ordained as a rabbi.*

5. *You became leader of a rabbinic school.*

6. *You were crowned King of Israel.*

All of these were major life changes and none were likely to happen to Nicodemus now due to his age. Imagine his surprise. What did Jesus mean? What options were left? Was he to re-enter his mother's womb?

What exactly was Jesus emphasizing? What was His message? What did He say next?

> *"Very truly I tell you, no one can enter the Kingdom of God unless they are born of water and the Spirit."*[23]

And the *Spirit*.

The six uses of 'born again' were rituals of some sort.

Consummation

Ordination

Coronation

But Jesus was emphasizing that a ceremony could not save you. His message seemed to challenge the idea that it was just something you simply went through once. Jesus was getting at something else, something to do with the Spirit.

I believe in justification by faith, but this fresh understanding made me question if I had led people to believe that just a moment of faith is required. Following Jesus is not about a moment of faith but a lifestyle of faith . . . a lifestyle that sets its sights higher than rules and looks to the Spirit behind them.

Had I missed His context and encouraged people to think they are born again simply because they went through a modern Protestant evangelical ceremony? How should this better understanding of Jesus' message affect my methods?

It is the Spirit, not a ritual, which reproduces Jesus in our lifestyle.

And the Spirit' is the key to a life of faith.

Without the Spirit, we accept an invitation to the wrong party. Jesus' context requires me to ask the question, "Am I in danger of simply adding number seven to the list of rituals?"

> 7. *Putting your hand up in the air after an altar call.*

In this case at least, seven is not a lucky number.

Delay

Sometimes Jesus confuses me.

Consider, for instance, the account of Lazarus' death recorded in John 11. When Jesus is told that His friend is seriously sick, He seems at first hard-hearted, apathetic, or at best, distracted. Rather than rushing to Lazarus' aid, Jesus delays His trip for a couple of days, arriving after the man has died and been entombed.

Why delay? Why create more anxiety than needed? Why allow His friends to feel pain? Why encourage doubt?

Specifically, the Bible tells us Lazarus had been entombed for four days.[24]

This is significant.

The Bible does not contain any FYI's.

If it is specific, it is significant!

The Pharisees taught and many Jews believed that the spirit hovered over a dead body for three days. It was believed that a person could be 'resuscitated' within that time. Even today there are often medical reports of people 'dying' for minutes on a surgeon's table but then coming back to life. The Jews therefore even had a custom called *Shiv'ah* meaning 'seven.' The mourners would mourn very heavily for the first three days, then heavily for the next four, and then lightly for the rest of the month. These first three days were intensely sorrowful but laced with hope.[25]

Jesus had raised people from the dead soon after their death and so had other Biblical heroes, but in Jewish history no one had been raised from the dead after four days.[26] After researching various sources for a better understanding of the context, I discovered that the Jews believed that only the Messiah could do this!

Jesus delayed in order to heal after the fourth day, but why?

To create understanding of *whom* He was, not simply *what* He could do.

I realized through the *intended* level that sometimes Jesus delays His answer to my prayers because what is more important than an answer is *understanding* the answer.

Kosher

The best way to study the Word of God is to be driven by questions. The biggest and most important question is, "What is His word trying to teach us about the heart of God?"

Soon after the birth of the Church, something very unexpected happened. The Gentiles were born again and filled with the Spirit, and the disciples saw this as a seal upon their lives. They realized that God had a plan for these new 'Christians,' and they reported their findings to the Council of Jerusalem.

Soon afterwards, some of the Pharisees demanded that these new converts be circumcised and be required to obey the Law of Moses. The Council, therefore, had a problem. What advice should they give them? What instructions? They spent some time discussing and seeking discernment from the Holy Spirit, and then they simply declared:

> *It seemed good to the Holy Spirit and to us not to burden you with anything beyond the following requirements: You are to abstain from food sacrificed to idols, from blood, from the meat of strangled animals and from sexual immorality. You will do well to avoid these things.*[27]

So what on earth can that divine command teach today's Christian about God and what He desires?

The *intended* meaning encouraged me to ask the following questions:

1. Were these the only commandments that these Gentiles needed to observe?

2. Why was such importance placed on the food laws? Why not emphasize many of the other Laws of Moses?

When I ask most Christians what they think the Jews believed about the Gentiles and if they could be saved, the general response is that they had not really thought about it before. Some thought that the Jews believed the Gentiles could not be saved; others suggested that the Gentiles would have to convert to Judaism. Both of these answers make sense when you skim the surface of the Bible without even delving into the first level of context.

But here is what I discovered at the first level of HD . . .

For a very long time, well before this story in Acts, the Jews believed that the Gentiles could be part of *Olam Haba*, the world to come, a Jewish euphemism for what we might call Heaven. In Jesus' day, such Gentiles were known as 'God-fearers,' and they were given a place in the temple called the Court of the Gentiles. The God-fearers would commit to the Noahide Laws.[28] These laws, listed by the *Tosefta* and the *Talmud*, originated in Genesis 9.

> *Prohibition of idolatry*
>
> *Prohibition of murder*
>
> *Prohibition of theft*
>
> *Prohibition of sexual immorality*
>
> *Prohibition of blasphemy*
>
> *Prohibition of eating flesh taken from an animal while it is still alive*
>
> *Establishment of courts of law*

So when James stood up at the Council of Jerusalem, it was already understood that these new converts would need to live by the Noahide Laws. That's my first question answered.

But why emphasize the particular food restrictions that added to them?

This question leads us to understand something very important about God's heart for His people. This additional emphasis prompted by the Spirit was given so that the Gentiles could sit down to a meal and break bread with their Jewish brothers who would otherwise be restricted socially because of the Law of Moses.

The *intended* level helps me understand that even though the Gentiles did not have to obey the food restrictions to obey the law of God, they did it to please the heart of God. God, they realized, sees our commitment to Him through our commitment to His body. We cannot reflect His glory simply as individuals; only in community can we fully give testimony that He is indeed the God that is Love.

P'shat means 'simple.'

It is just the beginning.

How?

Irony

To make Jesus' words fully relevant to our culture, we must perhaps first understand *His*. Doing so may help us filter out any misdirection given to us by our own.

A true commitment to the *intended* meaning will protect us from the temptation to which we are all prone—the temptation to cut and paste scripture in a way that will best promote our personal agenda. Perhaps most importantly, however, it provides a safety net for all the adventure, excitement, and freedom that comes from exploring the deeper levels. Or as the rabbis put it:

> "No scripture ever loses its *p'shat*." [29]

In other words, this *intended* meaning stops us from coming up with crazy interpretations of scripture when we engage in some of the more flamboyant and creative exercises.

So how exactly do we, as a Haverim, study at this level?

Questions

In my Haverim, because of its size, after we read a passage of scripture, we split into smaller groups. Each group answers two types of questions.

Some questions are *generic* and some are *specific*.

The *generic* questions apply to all passages:

> Who wrote it?
>
> Why did they write it?
>
> Where were they when they wrote it?
>
> How is it affected by other customs of the day?
>
> What happened before or after the incident in the life of the person who wrote it or the people it was about?
>
> What can archaeology teach us about this passage?
>
> What does history teach us about the subject?

The specific questions vary and are determined by the overall thought that the Haverim wants to look at. The guiding question will be phrased by the Haverim teacher and will lead the group in its journey to discover the *intended* meaning of a passage. For instance, my Haverim recently discussed John's question of Jesus:

> *"Are you really the one?"*[30]

One of the facets I hoped the group would eventually discover was that if we truly wish to seek first the Kingdom of God, we will need to trust Him even when He does things differently from what we would like.

So to get us going at the *intended* level, the *specific* questions relating to context were:

> What was John's relationship to Jesus?
>
> What had he already said about Jesus?
>
> What does history tell us happened to John?
>
> What does history tell us eventually happened to the disciples sent by John?

Often, I will have some groups look at the generic questions and a couple of the other groups look at the specific questions. The groups will spend about thirty minutes together and then report back to discuss their findings.

Importantly, I rarely organize people to research by themselves. Why? So that newbies will not feel exposed, and so that one person can train another younger, less experienced or less mature member how to study.

Tools

We equip our groups with a variety of tools to search out their answers.

Obviously, if you are leading a group of Haverim, you may want to initially provide these resources for your friends with the hope that they will learn how to use them and begin to resource themselves.

Even as I am writing this, I know that my recommendations are quickly becoming outdated because many people in the Haverim on my street bring commentaries that are online and read them on their smartphones or tablets. Everything I list below can now be carried with you if you are fortunate enough to own one of these devices. Not only is it more practical to carry these books digitally, it is far less intimidating for those who do not own the books or are unfamiliar with them.

The following recommendations are generic. I am hoping that on the website we can share our favorite resources.[31] Depending on whether or not you are pioneering a Haverim group, taking part in one, or simply attempting to use the four levels of HD in your own personal study, these seven tools are ideal for discovering the *intended* meaning of a passage. They are certainly not the only ones, and I would encourage you not to limit the allowed resources in any way.

Commentary

> A commentary is an interpretation of a passage. It may be based on a particular book or the entire Bible. A commentary may contain studies of words, phrases, history, parables, etc. In addition to the author's interpretation, it also brings contextual information to the passage.

> There are roughly two types of commentary. The first is a commentary within a Bible. In the past, I have used the *NIV Study Bible* and

the *NLT Life Application Study Bible*, which both contain commentary on the Bible passages as you read them. These two study Bibles come from different perspectives. The first gives more factual information and the second offers observations on how you might apply a passage to yourself. Presently, I use the *NIV Archaeological Study Bible* which comments on the history and culture of the passages.

The other type of commentary is a stand-alone one. These can come as individual books or as a series. To be honest, commentaries are like a piece of string; they can go on forever. My advice is that when you are gathering as a Haverim, depending on the situation, you may not wish to bring too many books; the first type of commentary (one contained within the Bible) plus online commentaries on your phone may be the best way forward.[32]

Encyclopedia

One particular type of handbook that I have found ideal for understanding context is a Biblical encyclopedia.[33] Some are specific to historical facts and archaeology. For the visually driven like myself, these books are extremely useful. They can usually be browsed by timeline and/or topic. Sometimes the information they throw out is a little pointless but adds color. Did you know, for instance, that popcorn was a staple diet for many people in Biblical days? Other information, however, vastly improves my understanding of a story, place, or person, and affects how I see even the simplest passage of scripture.

Concordance

A concordance allows me to find a particular word or phrase, and then it lists the many passages of scripture in which that word is also found. Again, this simple tool gives me the benefit of understanding. So let's say God uses a peculiar phrase to describe someone. A concordance can show me other instances where the phrase is used in the Bible. These other instances lead me to a fuller realization and appreciation of what He meant. As with commentaries, you can find concordances within your Bible or as standalone books. In the past, I have used *Gruden's Complete Concordance to the Old and New Testaments*, but today I often use biblegateway.com as it provides not only an instant comprehensive list, but gives me the option to find the word in other translations.

Topical

A topical Bible or book brings out cultural and historical background about specific topics. Like encyclopedias, these books are useful for understanding parables, details about certain jobs, techniques, manners, or customs, and so much more. They come in all shapes and sizes. Some cover the entire Bible and others target specific topics. One of these books gave me a completely different perspective on how Jesus used parables; it helped me understand that in some cases, he was not simply creating a new story but reshaping an existing one in order to emphasize what was truly important to the Father.[34]

Unlike some other resources, specific topical books are only brought to the Haverim when specific passages are being examined. So if we were studying Psalm 23 with a theme of shepherding, we would bring topical books that cover that kind of career.

Translations

Each translation of the Bible has a particular emphasis, and different insights can be gained by the different wording. Unlike most church services, which encourage people to quite literally be on the same page by reading the same version, in a Haverim group it is very useful for different people to bring different versions. This not only benefits us in the *intended* level but the *interpreted* level as well.

Certain Bibles make it easy to compare different translations by placing them together. These are called Parallel Bibles. Again, the invention of online Bibles and apps means that with the flick of a thumb you can switch translations and compare them.

Dictionary

Occasionally, a dictionary of difficult words or doctrines can be useful. Certain passages benefit greatly from this type of book if you are trying to understand peculiar or unfamiliar phrases in their context, particularly in the epistles. If you remember, the *intended* level is our safety net. These books help ensure that we do not create a false theological perspective from an isolated comment or instruction because we are unfamiliar with the framework in which it is set.

Digital

As I have said, there are many digital versions of all the above, most of which are free on the internet or as apps. In addition, online resources encompass many, if not all of them. A good Haverim leader will keep seeking these out and passing them on to the group.

The other benefit of digital resources is that they can easily be shared via Twitter or Facebook. We have created a Facebook group for our Haverim to share the things we find.

Not everyone will enjoy this *intended* level as much as they will enjoy the others, but it is without a doubt the one that gives us the foundation. It is like setting up a base camp at the foot of a mountain; it provides everything we need to go further and everything we require for our journey to stay on track.

Implied

R'mez

Why?

Shallow

Picture the possibility of discovering hidden treasures buried in God's Word.

> *"Some fell on rocky places, where it did not have much soil. It sprang up quickly, because the soil was shallow. But when the sun came up, the plants were scorched, and they withered because they had no root."*[35]

Ever felt that your understanding of God was shallow?

Ever felt that you've followed God for shallow reasons?

Maybe there is a connection.

A story is told of the Prince of Grenada who was locked away in prison for many years. Granted one request, he asked to be given a Bible and spent the entire time of incarceration alone with this one book. When he died, it was noted that the walls of his cell were filled with Bible trivia:

Psalm 118:8 is the middle verse of the Bible.

Ezra 7:21 contains all the letters of the alphabet except the letter J.

Esther 8:9 is the longest verse in the Bible.

No word or name with more than six syllables is found in scripture.

It was said of the prince that he knew a book that never *changed* him.

His captors saw no sign in his behavior that its words had taken root, because the Bible without understanding is full of lessons that can never be learned.

Why? Because we do not see the *connections*.

We don't spend the time or know the techniques to spot the spiritual synergy flowing through it.

> *Parables compel listeners to discover truth, while at the same time concealing the truth from those too lazy or stubborn to see it.* [36]

I recently heard the word 'genius' described as 'the ability to see patterns between isolated facts.'

This is surely the key to spiritual wisdom. This is the kind of wisdom that Jesus passed on to His disciples. He gave *patterns* and *principles* to those eager enough to find them. He filtered out those who were looking for easy answers in order to manipulate God, while the seekers of the Kingdom were equipped not simply to know what to do in a certain situation, but with understanding of how to determine God's will for any situation.

The second level of Haverim Devotions™ will empower us with that kind of wisdom. It will help us find the *connections* required to comprehend God's *principles*.

When I teach the second level of HD, I show a selection of artwork. I present three paintings from one artist, then three from another, and finally three paintings from a third. Then I present a final painting from one of the three. No matter how little my audience knows about art, and even though they have never seen this particular painting before, they instantly know who the artist is. They know because they have seen a pattern emerge. And this pattern, this way of painting, this recognition of style allows them to easily spot the hand of the artist.

So it is with the Word of God.

The Bible becomes much more than spiritual graffiti.

What?

Connection

The second level of Haverim Devotions™ is the *implied* meaning.

The *implied* meaning gives us the clues to something hidden in the passage.

The Hebrew word for this second level is *r'mez* and means 'hint.'

The method of the *implied* meaning is to seek *connections*.

R'mez is where scripture interprets scripture. The Bible comes to our aid when it equips us with patterns of why what happened happens. If we miss its riddles, we miss the deeper values that God has to teach us. This is where we have to make a decision: do we only want to learn *what* to think or are we eager to understand *how* to think?

If we miss His connections, we miss His principles.

The reason is not because we do not know they are there, but because we do not know how to find them.

To go to this next level in a passage, we ask:

What previous story, passage, or prophecy is this connected to?

Is the writer referring to another biblical incident, story, or prophecy?

Are they bringing our attention to a fuller meaning by hinting at something and invoking its message?

We intentionally look for a principle to be discovered or a pattern to be noticed. We ask, "Might we apply these principles and patterns to our life?" We wonder where else in scripture these principles and patterns were adhered to or ignored. What were the consequences?

We ask, "How does the dynamic of *r'mez* teach us more than just a comparison?"

To help us understand *r'mez*, here are some principles the *implied* meaning taught me.

Sticks

On the cross, Jesus utters these mortal words:

> *"My God, My God, why have you forsaken me?"*[37]

So many questions.

For many years, I struggled with this. Why did Jesus believe that God had forsaken Him? Had God forsaken Him? What was going on?

I understand the usual answers—that the sin of the world was put on Jesus and God turned away from Him. This answer, however, just leads me to more questions.

At what point does sin get so bad that God will turn His face from us forever? Is there a place where we cross over a line and God forsakes us? Why did Jesus clearly believe that He would rise again and yet now declare that God had given up on Him? Was Jesus confused?

And most importantly, the question that nobody ever answers is this . . .

Why did Jesus say, *"Why?"*

If the Father had forsaken Him, wouldn't the Son of God simply have cried:

> *"My God, My God, you have forsaken me!"*

The answer lies not in the *simple* message but in the *hinted* message.

To explain, let me first help you understand the dynamics of *r'mez* that Jesus is invoking here upon the cross. Imagine one day I am speaking somewhere and a gentleman shouts out, "Paul, you bore me and you have an ugly face!" I might simply say in return:

"Sticks and stones, sir, sticks and stones."

Every Englishman knows exactly what I am implying. I am saying the first three words of a well-known children's rhyme:

Sticks and stones may break my bones,
But words will never hurt me.

By citing the first line of this familiar saying, I am invoking its whole meaning to my audience. The Englishman realizes that I will not be taking his words to heart.

However, what about the Germans in the room?

Few foreigners know the saying that I have only partially quoted, and so they might interpret my words very differently. They may even create a doctrine based on the importance of standing up for yourself and threatening violence when you are insulted—all based upon my words, "sticks and stones." This is one of the dangers of skimming the surface of scripture. We come up with 'biblical' doctrines that may fit into our worldview, but not God's.

When Jesus is on the cross, He is quoting the first verse of Psalm 22.

Now some people may have realized that, but they rarely understand the dynamic that Jesus was using. On the cross, He is not simply quoting a memory verse; He is doing something far more profound. Christ is bringing to life the whole of the Psalm! He is essentially declaring the whole of its message to be true and fulfilled before their eyes. Jesus is invoking *r'mez*.

Psalm 22 starts off with: *My God, My God, why have you forsaken me?*

But this poem, which was approximately one thousand years old at the time of the crucifixion, also includes the following staggering remarks:

I am poured out like water, and all my bones are out of joint [...] My strength is dried up like a potsherd, and my tongue sticks to the roof of my mouth; you lay me in the dust of death. Dogs surround me, a pack of villains encircles me; they pierce my hands and my feet. All my bones are on display; people stare and gloat over me. They divide my clothes among them and cast lots for my garment. [38]

On the hill at Calvary when Jesus cried out these words, a filtering process occurred. Those simply following the Son of God for the sake of food, healing, and escape from their Roman overlords would have just walked away from that hill disappointed that they did not get from Jesus what they had come to expect.

However, some may have had ears to hear.

How the hairs on their necks must have stood up when they realized that King David's prophecy was coming to pass before their very eyes! Water *was* pouring out of his side as a Roman soldier pierced it with a spear, his bones *were* dislocated as He was raised and lowered on the stake and His clothes *had* been divided among the guards. If they were truly seeking the Kingdom of God, how their hearts would also have beaten faster when Jesus' shout brought to mind what He was really getting at . . . the following verses from the rest of the Psalm:

You who fear the Lord, praise him! Revere him, all you descendants of Israel! For he has not despised or disdained the suffering of the afflicted one; he has not hidden his face from him but has listened to his cry for help. All the ends of the earth will remember and turn to the Lord [...] those who cannot keep themselves alive. Posterity will serve him; future generations will be told about the Lord. They will proclaim his righteousness, declaring to a people yet unborn: He has done it. [39]

'He has done it' or, in other words: "It is finished."

Jesus was not forsaken!

Jesus would be rescued!

And all of this would have a greater purpose. It would bring future generations and different nations to Him and change the world as they knew it!

For me, the *implied* meaning challenges my soul. It teaches me a principle as I connect the story of Jesus' death to King David's Psalm. I realize that God is looking for those who will not simply follow Him because He fulfills their individual immediate needs, but instead He longs for those who long for His ultimate, intimate plan. And those who do so will have their individual intimate needs met if they put His first.

It forces me to ask myself the question, "Would I have just walked away thinking, *It's over, this guy is not who I thought he was?*" Or, would my heart have been leaning forward, amazed, intrigued, and excited by the message of Psalm 22?

All of this from one verse that many of us skip over even though deep down we know there's something very odd about it.

Blessed

The *implied* meaning takes many forms, but most of them hint at something unsaid.

When John the Baptist, Jesus' cousin, is in prison, it seems he begins to wrestle with all kinds of doubts about Jesus' identity. At one point, he finally sends some of his disciples to his relative to ask the question:

> *Are you the one who is to come, or should we expect someone else?*[40]

Jesus' reply at first seems like a straight forward answer:

> *Jesus replied, "Go back and report to John what you hear and see: The blind receive sight, the lame walk, those who have leprosy are cleansed, the deaf hear, the dead are raised, and the good news is proclaimed to the poor."*[41]

He lists some of His extraordinary acts, but then, He completes it with an enigmatic conclusion:

52

"Blessed is anyone who does not stumble on account of me." [42]

What has this last phrase got to do with anything? How could John possibly fall away from Jesus? And in what way would he be blessed if he did not?

In Jesus' reply to John's disciples, He is invoking to their minds the seven works that the Jews were expecting of the Messiah based upon the prophecies of Isaiah:

He will make the blind to see. (Isaiah 28:18)

He will make the lame walk. (Isaiah 35:6 & 61:1)

He will cleanse lepers. (Isaiah 53:4)

He will make the deaf hear. (Isaiah 29:18 & 35:5)

He will raise the dead. (Isaiah 11:1-2)

He will evangelize the poor. (Isaiah 61:1)

He will set the prisoners free. (Isaiah 61:1)

These specific miracles were the litmus test or measurement with which the Jews would compare any pseudo-messiah. The Sanhedrin used this list of seven wonders when sending a posse of religious leaders to check up on any claims of candidacy for Messiahship.

Jesus lists the things He has done, but what do you notice?

With *r'mez* sometimes what you don't say is more powerful than what you do say. What I notice is this: Jesus only points to six of the seven prophetic acts. He leaves one out.

Can you guess which one?

When John's disciples approach, Jesus has already read the heart of the one who sent them. By invoking *r'mez*, John's cousin lets him know two important things:

Yes, I am the Messiah, but no, I will not be setting you free!

Then He also assures John that if he does not fall away because of the *way in which He does things*, he will be especially blessed.

The *intended* meaning gives me the context of the seven prophecies; it helps me understand that Jesus is relaying six of Isaiah's prophecies. But, it is only when I understand the *r'mez* that the *implied* meaning communicates God's principle to me: The Lord puts the Kingdom before my personal concerns.

He has a plan that I may not understand, but if I also put His Kingdom first, then I can trust that, in the eternal scheme of things, I will be blessed and given all I really need and so much more.

Touch

The key to the *implied* meaning may be hidden in what is said or what is unsaid, but also in what is done:

> *And a woman was there who had been subject to bleeding for twelve years. She had suffered a great deal under the care of many doctors and had spent all she had, yet instead of getting better, she grew worse. When she heard about Jesus, she came up behind him in the crowd and touched his cloak, because she thought, "If I just touch his clothes, I will be healed." Immediately her bleeding stopped and she felt in her body that she was freed from her suffering.* [43]

The simplistic English phrasing of this story does the woman an injustice. Jewish Messianic writers, however, teach us significant details about what actually happened. Importantly, they tell us that the woman with the issue of blood reached and touched the *tassels* in the corner of His robe.

Why? Because Malachi prophesied that the Messiah would come with healing in His 'wings.' [44]

Wings were a name also given to the tassels on a rabbi's clothing. [45]

She believed the prophecy. She had connected what she saw of Jesus with the words of the prophet whose prophecy had authority in her life.

The *hint* came first; the *healing* came afterwards.

Stamps

I collect *r'mez* in the same way that some people collect stamps.

Jesus was very good at speaking in parables but uniquely gifted at hinting. An estimated fifty *r'mez* are recorded within Jesus' words in the four gospels and countless more are in the rest of the Bible. The genius of Jesus is that He was able to say things without saying them. This not only helped Him avoid being trapped by His accusers, but more importantly it helped people really get what He was communicating.

As we discover more of the *context* of the Bible, so the potential of discovering more *connections* grows. The more connections you can unearth, the more exciting Bible study becomes.

Like stamps, *r'mez* share an attribute that most of us could emulate:

> They stick to one thing until they get there.

How?

Filter

Why can't the Bible just be simple? Why must its authors and its participants hint at things when they could have simply come out and said them?

As previously quoted, parables compel listeners to discover truth, while at the same time concealing the truth from those too stubborn or lazy to see it. You could also say this about many scriptures that are not contained within the parables.

Why? Maybe it is for the same reason Jesus chose His disciples.

Oddly, He did not choose from the crowds sitting at His feet, but from those who were still talking, working, and washing their nets.

I'm not sure I would have done that. At least a few years ago, I would have been more impressed with those hanging onto my words on the shore of Galilee with their minds open and punching into their iPads every word of wisdom dropping from my lips. I would not have chosen those I saw from the corner of my eyes going about their daily business perhaps only half listening to me. How rude!

Years later, however, I think I am beginning to get it.[46] The fishermen were sticking with something they knew to be a process; they were fulfilling something they had promised to do. They were not displaying a *moment* of commitment, but a *lifestyle* of commitment. Even though a famous Rabbi was nearby and as much as they surely would have loved to rest and be entertained by His stories, they stuck to what they should be doing.

Jesus is not looking for a *fickle* audience, but a *faithful* one—a gathering of those keen to stick with something until it yields a reward.

Is that you?

Would you like that to be you? Because it will involve wrestling, won't it? It will require a desire for truth, and truth comes at a price, doesn't it? Unlike the dog in the film *Up!* that is distracted every time it thinks it sees a squirrel, we cannot jump from one titillating soundbite to another. Instead, we must pursue the heart of God. Ironically, though, that may involve following Him down some hidden trails because the Bible is not structured to be simple but to offer surprises, twists, and turns in order to see who follows its path.

It seems to me that the Bible is a filter.

Questions

In my Haverim, we study both the *intended* and *implied* meanings together because they are similar in that they are research-based. If you also put these two stages together, the *implied* meaning will use the same tools but different questions.

This second stage analyzes the level of people's perceptions. A good Haverim teacher or student will encourage the genius of making connections. The value of seeing what at first cannot be seen and the struggle to dig deeper than the obvious should be commended.

Again, *generic* questions and *specific* questions are posed.

The *generic* questions are:

Does the passage refer to another incident, story, or prophecy in the Bible?

Does anything referenced here have a meaning elsewhere in scripture?

Remember that at this level we are looking for principles and patterns. Once the context had been discovered in John's question of Jesus, we asked questions that helped us get where we needed to go.

The *specific* questions might be ones such as:

> Is there a principle to be discovered or a pattern to be noticed?
>
> How might these principles and patterns be applied to situations in our lives?
>
> What other places in scripture were these principles applied and ignored?
>
> What were the consequences?

In my particular Haverim during the first night of study, we may have four small groups of people looking at the four different types of questions: the generic and specific for the *intended* meaning and also for the *implied* meaning. This can lead to a wealth of new information rather than simply restating things we already knew.

So how do we find these implications in scripture?

Implications

Verses

> The most basic form of *r'mez* is cross-referencing. We make a connection to a reference in another part of the Bible, read its context, and see if we can find a hint of a wider message.
>
> Some of the *r'mez* I pointed out were ones you could have seen for yourself. They were hidden in the cross-references of most Bibles, but many of us are just not interested enough to check them out because we don't realize the dynamic sometimes being used.

Phrases

> Look for a phrase that stands out in the scripture you are studying. In the same way as Jesus' statement on the cross is found in Psalm 22,

does this phrase appear in other places in the Bible? Is one referencing another?

An added aspect of this is the law of 'first reference,' which means that if you can find the very first time that verse appears, you may see something at which the writer is hinting.

Names

When a name of a place or a person comes up, see if it is connected to its appearance elsewhere in scripture. Discover the story behind the other references and explore any hints that may be suggesting a deeper truth. The scripture you are studying may be brought to life through the context of the scripture to which it is connected.

Numbers

Most numbers in the Bible have significance. If you notice when Jesus reminds His disciples of the feeding of the 4,000 and 5,000, He points to two specific numbers—not the amount of people fed, but, oddly, the amount of baskets left over.

When the feeding of the 5,000 was performed in Galilee, twelve baskets were recovered, yet when in another area, only seven baskets were left over. There is something about these numbers that Jesus felt was important for His disciples to grasp. There was a clue to something they had not yet realized.

The *Hasidim* referred to the land where the feeding of 5,000 took place in the land of Israel, but the Hellenistic cities of the Decapolis were referred to as the land of the seven. Using a number-based *r'mez*, Jesus is saying to them that He is the bread of life both to the Jews and the Gentiles.

Places

The *implied* meaning can help us see beyond the words and help us sense something of what God actually feels. Not only are the words not said as important as those that are said, but also *where* they are said can have huge implications.

Famously, before His arrest, Jesus goes to the garden of Gethsemane on the Mount of Olives, and during the evening, He utters these incredible words:

> *"Father, if you are willing, take this cup from me; yet not my will, but yours be done."* [47]

There are two *r'mez* in this verse, but I will just share one with you. The six middle words are shocking:

> *". . . yet not my will, but yours . . ."*

This is the only time in the Bible that we see the Son's will as different from the Father's.

I had never noticed that until a member of an HD group pointed it out. Up until then, maybe because I always knew what happened next, I just thought Jesus was going through the motions—as though His will and the Father's were so inseparable that His crucifixion was *fated* to happen.

But one *r'mez* brings this passage to life. It adds tension, drama, and most importantly, a better sense of Jesus' sacrificial state-of-mind. You see, in the prophecy of Zechariah, it is said that the Mount of Olives will split and the valley that God creates there will be used by the people as an *escape route* from their enemies. [48]

It is here, in this chosen place that Jesus asked to be delivered. Had He gone here to remind His Father of the prophecy? Was Jesus hinting at something? Was it here that Jesus was hoping to escape if the Father willed it?

Some might say this is pure coincidence.

Is it?

If you have a heart to understand, you will notice that a few moments earlier Jesus had quoted from the predictions of Zechariah:

> *I will strike the shepherd, and the sheep of the flock will be scattered.* [49]

There is no doubt in my mind that this prophecy was on *His* mind. Jesus was not just flippantly going through the motions, requesting something He knew could never happen. This was a genuine request!

Jesus had options. He was taken to the very brink of temptation. He really was asking the Father to take His destiny away, but something in the moment stopped Jesus from demanding an alternative path. Places are significant. Often, there is an implication and a lesson to be learned. In this case, the *implied* meaning helps me see Jesus modeling a principle close to His heart:

To advance the Kingdom, we must live by *faith* not by *fate*.

Leaders

For the *implied* meaning to work, the leader must remind those involved of the three things needed.

First, the hearer must first know the context.

Secondly, they must be spiritually keen enough to make connections.

Thirdly, the hearer must actually believe the fuller message for the hint to carry any weight. For instance, if the 'sticks and stones' analogy were ever really used, it would not only fail with those who have never heard the full poem, but also with someone who *does* believe that words *can* harm us.

The *implied* level therefore requires two things:

> The *faithfulness* to look for a deeper message,
> and the *faith* to believe in it.

INTERPRETED

D'rash

Why?

Space

Visualize a life in which you have the freedom to grasp all God has spoken to you.

"Other seed fell among thorns, which grew up and choked the plants."[50]

Ever felt that your understanding of God lacked space for other ideas?

Ever felt that your religion lacked space to do God's will?

Maybe there is a connection.

Some of us are bored with the Word of God because all we hear are the same old clichés. I have often wondered: Where are the *unique* explanations? Where is the gap for *innovative* ideas?

Will there ever be room for the *new* to sit with the *old*? It seems they are destined to attack each other for all time.

Why? Because we don't know how to *collaborate*.

> He said to them, "Therefore every teacher of the law who has become a disciple in the kingdom of heaven is like the owner of a house who brings out of his storeroom new treasures as well as old."[51]

It has been said that a parable compares something familiar to something unfamiliar, the familiar being material and the unfamiliar being spiritual.

Jesus would point to something everybody recognized and knew in order to explain something they did not recognize and had not known.

So my question is, if each one of us sees the material things differently, can the spiritual lessons be different as well? If so, is that why it takes a community to search out scripture? Is that why one person interpreting for everyone else is dangerous?

We all see from different angles.

Take a look at the diagram below:

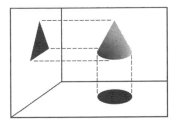

From one perspective, all you can see is a triangle; from another, all that is recognized is a circle. Not until both perspectives are united is the recognition of a full cone seen by all. Truth is not one-dimensional; it is at least three-dimensional.

Now look at this second illustration:

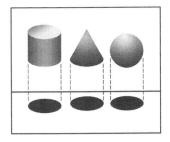

Three very different objects are viewed from only one perspective. This singular viewpoint dumbs down the variety, objectivity, and possibility of what is really there.

The idea that one man or woman should speak and interpret scripture for everyone will always choke the dream of the Kingdom of Heaven.

The third level of Haverim Devotions™ will teach us how to avoid just that. It will help us find the *collaboration* required to comprehend God's *purpose*— not because that one perspective is necessarily wrong; it is just terribly, terribly incomplete.

The sages said, "Every scripture has seventy facets." [52]

Seventy is the number that represents infinity. Of course there are dangers in this, as I will discuss later, but authentic study must take this risk. In the days of Jesus, it *always did*, and in our emerging world, it *always must*.

In our Haverim, we can move from *one-to-many* to *many-to-many*.

In our Haverim, we can move from *exclusivity* to *inclusivity*.

In our Haverim, we can move from trusting in a *system* to trusting in the *Spirit*.

We can move from a community that is less polarized and travel toward one that seeks perfection in perception. And, it will allow us to invite some unusual travelers along the way—ones who could not journey with us in our old vehicle because they were at best a passenger, but now they can happily step on board as a participator.

Just like the cone, ball, and cylinder, together we can all gain spiritual depth-perception.

What?

Collaboration

The third level of Haverim Devotions™ is the *interpreted* meaning.

The *interpreted* meaning offers perspectives that fill the gaps in a passage.

The Hebrew word for this level is *d'rash* and means 'search.'

The method of the *interpreted* meaning is to seek *collaboration*.

To go to this next level, more than asking questions, we *become* the question. We engage ourselves in the passage by embedding ourselves within it. *Midrash* was an ancient way of interpreting a passage by filling in the gaps. It brings together what is familiar to each one of us, in order to see what is unfamiliar to every one of us.

If *r'mez* is where we let scripture interpret scripture, *d'rash* is where scripture interprets motive. Before we simply read the Bible, now the Bible reads us. In doing so, it helps us understand our hopes and fears, His hopes and dreams.

If we miss the collaboration, we miss His purpose—not because we cannot find purpose, but because we only see it from one angle . . . usually our own.

When we examine at a passage at this level, we ask questions such as:

> What is the motive behind what was said or done?

We then look at one or two verses that contain the key to the message. We create our *midrash*, a certain type of interpretation, by adhering to the following instructions:[53]

> Tell the story, fill in the gaps,
> but whatever you do, don't change the facts.

The *interpreted* passage is, for some, the most dynamic and freeing of all four levels. It appeals especially to those who love learning not just about God but others, and it creates an adventure of unlimited possibilities. At the *interpreted* level, we can also discover more about what limits our relationship with God and what could take it to a new level.

Rather than me teaching you the lessons I have learned from this level, let me help you learn your own.

Jehoash

Do you fully use all that is at your disposal?

If not, why not?

Within the Bible is a story of King Jehoash—not a very godly man, but a man who knew God.[54] He is facing the king of Aram and realizes that defeat is inevitable. In the course of a strange story, a prophet asks the king to perform two bizarre activities.

First he asks him to shoot an arrow through a window, and then he tells him to strike the ground with the arrows. The king, for reasons it does not say, only strikes the ground *three* times. The prophet, again for reasons not mentioned, is annoyed at the king, and after promising a full victory, now instead proclaims only a *half* victory.

Have you ever felt that you only get half-victories? Do you sometimes only half-heartedly use what God has given you? Why is that?

To help us understand his motive more fully, let me take you through the process of *d'rash*. To do this, we first look at the *intended* and *implied* levels, the *context* and the *connections*.

The *context* teaches me that Jehoash was an ungodly man, and that he was facing the king of Aram with what *The NIV Study Bible* describes as a 'small police force' for an army. He had inherited only ten chariots, fifty horsemen, and ten thousand soldiers. Bear in mind that in 857 BC, Ahab had destroyed ten times as many foot soldiers in one day of battle!

Secondly, context teaches us the meaning of Jehoash's statement when he met with the prophet Elisha:

> "My father, my father, the chariots and horseman of Israel!"[55]

This also may seem like one of those peculiar phrases we skip because we don't understand. However, it has significance to the story. Ancient Hebrews describe things differently from those in the modern western world. When we describe something, we usually comment on its *decorative* state, but the ancient Hebrews would describe something by its *function*. Even when a color was mentioned, it was symbolic because the color itself had a function. I, as an Englishman, may describe a sofa from IKEA as white and contemporary, whereas an ancient Hebrew might describe it as sturdy and with space to seat three people.[56]

So when Jehoash approaches Elisha, he greets the prophet by declaring his *function*. He has realized that Elisha represents Israel's only significant military resource.

The *connections* are where we go next. When the prophet commands the king to shoot an arrow through the east window, he is *hinting* in advance to Jehoash the possibility of more than just a simple victory. He is using *r'mez* by invoking into the king's memory an ancient practice of declaring war.

In history, when one faction felt offended or aggrieved by another, it would sometimes declare an intention to go to war by throwing a spear or shooting an arrow into the enemy's territory. This signified thirty days for the enemy to put things right and avoid conflict.

Here we may discover a helpful principle implied elsewhere in scripture.[57] How do we know when a Godly influence comes into our lives? We know because it moves us from defense to attack!

So the story is that Jehoash, an ungodly man, recognizes the prophet as God's resource and understands that God is giving him an opportunity to move from a position of desperation to one of advancement. So, why is it that the following happens?

> Then he said, "Take the arrows," and the king took them. Elisha told him, "Strike the ground." He struck it three times and stopped. The man of God was angry with him and said, "You should have struck the ground five or six times; then you would have defeated Aram and completely destroyed it. But now you will defeat it only three times." [58]

To understand what was going on in the heart of Jehoash, I first told you the story, and then gave you context. Now let me give you the verse and question.

Please look at 2 Kings 13:18:

> Then he said, "Take the arrows," and the king took them. Elisha told him, "Strike the ground." He struck it three times and stopped.

The question is:

> Why did Jehoash only strike the ground three times?

To discover the lessons for yourself, I invite you to:

> Retell the story, fill in the gaps,
> but whatever you do, don't change the facts.

In no more than three sentences, I would like you to tell the story from Jehoash's point of view. It is important that you speak in first person. So for instance, "I picked up the arrows" not "he picked up the arrows."

You need to tell us what you were thinking when Elisha gives you the command. What was going on in your mind and heart when you struck the ground?

Create your *midrash* on the lines that follow.

_____

_____

_____

_____

Warning: It is *very* important that you do this exercise before you read on. If you skip this, you will lose the power of what is about to happen.

So, what conclusion did you arrive at? What was going on in Jehoash's mind? What was he feeling in his heart? Why did he recognize God's resource, but not use it to its fullest?

Based upon what you just wrote, what is your summary of Jehoash's reason for not striking the ground three times? Was it that he needed more instructions? Was it because he didn't know why and didn't see the point? Was it because no one told him he could strike the ground more than three times? Was it because he was impatient to finish this bit of nonsense so that the prophet would quickly give him the real answer to his problem?

Here are the two benefits:

1. If you were doing this in a Haverim, the combined perspectives give a fuller understanding of why people, especially your friends, don't use all at their disposal.

2. According to the ancient rabbis and sages before and after Jesus' day, what you wrote is the *possible* reason that Jehoash did not use God's resource, but it is the *probable* reason why you would not have.

Importantly, the rabbis are not suggesting that you would have done what Jehoash did; rather, the suggestion is simply that if you had, then this is probably why. The benefit of understanding your motive in virtual reality is that you can then protect yourself from it in real situations you face.

Is that true for you? When you look at your *d'rash*, does it help you understand why you don't use all that God puts at your disposal?

This ancient process helps us engage in the story in a way unfamiliar to most of us. It gives us the freedom to explore and is particularly engaging for those who may not know God in the way you do, because as long as the *p'shat* is not compromised, there is no right or wrong answer . . . only perspective.

Peter

Do we ever step out in faith?

If yes, why?

> *Immediately Jesus made the disciples get into the boat and go on ahead of him to the other side, while he dismissed the crowd [. . .] and the boat was already a considerable distance from land, buffeted by the waves because the wind was against it. Shortly before dawn, Jesus went out to them, walking on the lake. When the disciples saw him walking on the lake, they were terrified. "It's a ghost," they said, and cried out in fear. But Jesus immediately said to them: "Take courage! It is I. Don't be afraid."*[59]

As you know, Peter then stepped out of the boat.

If you are a person of peace, you are also a person of faith. You stepped out in the past, maybe you are doing so right now, yet sometimes you have not. What can you learn about the times you have stepped out that could help you in the future? Could immersing ourselves in that story help us understand what would give us faith to do what Peter did in other areas of our lives? Let's find out!

First, let me give you the verse and question.

Please look at Matthew 14:28-29:

> *"Lord, if it's you," Peter replied, "tell me to come to you on the water."*

"Come," he said.

Then Peter got down out of the boat, walked on the water and came toward Jesus."

Then answer the question:

Why did Peter step out of the boat?

Now, in first person and in no more than three sentences, retell the story, fill in the gaps, but whatever you do, don't change the facts.

_____

_____

_____

_____

What did you see?

Did Peter do it because his friends encouraged him to? Was it because he was in the habit of always walking towards Jesus? Did he do it just to prove the miraculous to those watching?

Whatever you wrote is a *possible* reason why Peter stepped out of the boat, but the *probable* reason why you would have.

Whatever the reason may be, your discoveries can empower you for the future. When you want to step out in some area of your life, you can make sure you put into place the things you now know will lift your levels of faith.

Wrestle

At its most dynamic, the *interpreted* level is an exercise in *theology* not *anthropology*.[60]

Being part of a Haverim will provoke your mind and challenge your heart to learn so many new things about yourself, but that is not its primary motive.

What floats my boat is the idea that you and I can learn to grasp what is in the heart of God and know Him more closely.

Recently, a member of my Haverim asked if we could look at the story of Jacob wrestling with a man of God. They wondered what this enigmatic story was all about and hoped it could teach us about our struggles with the Lord. For me, it represented an opportunity to explore what is in God's heart and mind when He forces us to wrestle instead of just teaching us clearly the lesson we need to learn.

During the first two stages, we discovered where Jacob was, what was going through his mind, quite a lot about his nature and history, and we came to different conclusions of who the man of mystery was that fought Jacob. However, instead of slipping into the story as Jacob, we put ourselves in the place of God Himself.

I gave the following scripture:

So Jacob was left alone, and a man wrestled with him till daybreak. [61]

Then I asked the following question:

Why did God ask the angel to specifically wrestle with Jacob; why not ask him to simply speak to Jacob or instruct him through an illustrative miracle?

To do this, I gave them the following simple exercise:

Write a letter from God to the angel telling him your thoughts on Jacob and why specifically you want him to fight with Jacob.

Again they put themselves in first person and kept their letter to around three sentences. The first sentence contained what they thought about Jacob, the second was exactly what they instructed the angel to do, and the third described what they hoped would be the benefit of the wrestling contest.

What would your *d'rash* be?

_____

_____

_____

_____

_____

_____

_____

_____

We found two benefits to this exercise.

First, our Haverim began to learn from each other's experiences a little more of why God brought those people we struggle with into our lives.

Secondly, we learned from the perspective of other people something about God's heart that may not have occurred to us if we had simply tackled this story on our own.

Knowing God and knowing ourselves ... The two most important discoveries in life.

How?

Levi

A few years ago, while helping a church that wanted to reach the young people of its community, I instigated a teaching series called *My Generation*. Based upon the discipleship practices of Jesus and with a desire to help train our youth in communicating their faith, the idea was simple: an adult and a young person they mentored would tag-team preach together.[62]

I had the pleasure of kicking off the series with my youngest son, Levi. We spent some time studying together the story of Abraham and Isaac and unpacking its principles, then at age twelve he stood on a stage set in the middle of the room and together we shared what we had learned to an eager audience of his peers and elders.[63]

He was fantastic.

We both discovered so much, plus he had a knack for communicating and a certain 'coolness' about his style of delivery. In fact, I got a greater response to that message from young and old than I had ever received for any other youth service in my life. More intergenerational partnerships followed, and we planned to use the format several times a year.

Then, out of the blue, we were asked to stop.

It was deemed too soon. The young people were too young and did not have a broad enough grip on the Bible to preach. Plus, it was argued that a sixteen year old would not want to listen to a twelve or thirteen year old.

That conversation was a turning point for me. The first part of the argument to cease and desist held a bizarre irony: were we really being asked to halt activities that trained young people on-the-job and replace it with a Bible study to teach them how Jesus trained His young disciples on-the-job?

To teach is to learn twice. [64]

Things grow in one of two ways: *control* or *culture*. The Kingdom of God can only truly be advanced through culture, a culture that is promoted by leadership, occasionally pruned, but never persecuted by it. This, of course, takes risk. All sorts of dangers can lie ahead, depending upon our legitimate fears or illegitimate insecurities.

What if those we train come to the wrong conclusions?

What if those we train come to the *right* conclusions?

What if those we train are poorer teachers than we are?

What if those we train are *better* teachers than we are?

Well, the only other option is control. We can sit people down, give them a worksheet to complete and make sure they fill in the blanks the way we tell them to. But will this get us to where God had in mind?

The answer is clearly *no*.

So if we are still holding on to that method, what does that tell us about our motives?

Questions

In my Haverim, the third level takes on a different feel from the first two in that the emphasis is on *relationship* rather than *research*.

This third stage encourages people to engage in order to go to the next level. The key to understanding how to think is to change the question—to ask *why* rather than *what*.

Uniquely, at this level, there is only one question, a *specific* one—one that aims to find the hidden or unstated motive within a passage.

The *specific* question is put within this specific order:

1. Once the passage is read, the context and connections are presented.[65]
2. A particular short section, usually one verse, is highlighted.
3. The specific question of motive and purpose is given.
4. Permission is given to retell the story and fill in the gaps, but not change the facts.
5. An exercise is presented as a vehicle to do this.

Remember that, at this level, we are looking for God's purpose, the reason He inspired someone to pass onto us the letter, story, poem, etc. Our hope is that, at the end of the exercise, we and our friends will have gained more understanding of God's heart rather than simply what He did or said. We also hope to be empowered in the future by understanding more of what motivates us to do good or evil.

A good Haverim teacher will not simply stop with what has been found, but will lead a search towards what can be *applied*.

The simple written exercise that I took you through is powerful enough, but creativity is vital. No matter how good something is, if it is repeatedly done with no variation, it can become cliché. We prefer to use a little extra effort and think creatively about how we *d'rash* a passage. So what kind of exercises might be used? And does this work for all types of scripture including its letters, poems, and prophecies?

Exercises

Here are just a few examples of the types of exercises we use to *d'rash* a passage.

Art

An alternative to simply writing is to create a simple form of art. At times I have asked people to draw the story on a piece of paper. After first having everyone write their *d'rash*, my wife has given out paper clips and asked people to manipulate them into a shape that depicts what the person may be thinking or feeling. With a more artistic approach, it is still important for people to retell the story using the method of *d'rash*. However, the practice of including some form of art brings variety and helps those who feel they don't have a way with words.

Drama

In a similar way, the retelling can take the form of a simple skit. Depending on the type of group you are working with, you may find this to be a fun and surprisingly revealing way of gaining perspective on a passage of scripture.

Many years ago, a school allowed me to teach their drama group on ways that drama communicates philosophy. I spoke about modern films; we watched movie clips and discussed how every producer and director is using art to communicate his or her way of thinking. Then I divided the class into groups and gave them each a parable to read, the punch line of its intended meaning (such as, *you reap what you sow*), a setting in which it had to take place (such as a bus stop or police station), and one object they had to include. I then instructed them to rewrite the parable in this modern setting in a way that revealed the motives of the characters. They were not allowed to say the punch line, but the rest of the class had to guess what it was.

I did this many times and was repeatedly shocked by how the Holy Spirit led these young people to understand the dynamics of what Jesus had been teaching.

By immersing themselves in the Word, they had engaged themselves with its Author.

Photography

In the western world at least, almost everyone has a camera on their phone. So, for a fairly shy and perhaps initially hesitant group, a photographic approach may open up hearts and minds. A group could be given a few minutes to create their *d'rash* privately. Then, when they have realized what is in the heart of a character, they could simply take a photo of something that best represents it.

When the Haverim regroups, they can show the photo to everyone and either explain why they took it or allow the group to guess the meaning. This latter option creates a two-tiered approach to interpretation that can be doubly effective.

Game

Sometimes simple games can be employed. Once I have told a story, I retell it, but this time I leave blanks and point to people in the room who must promptly fill in the gaps. If they take too long or repeat something already said, they are 'out.' Specifically the gaps that I leave are either something that is said, thought, or believed. The gaps represent things not already contained in the passage. For instance, I may retell the parable of the prodigal son employing gaps like this:

> There was a man who had two sons. The younger son thought to himself _____ and so said to his father, 'Father, give me my share of the estate.' So the man divided his property between his sons, saying to his wife _____. Not long after that . . .

At each blank, I would point to a Haverim member and they would have to quickly respond. This is great once people have understood how the *interpreted* level works, because it gets their immediate response. It does not give them time to coach their thinking for feelings.

Comic

If you have time to prepare, then perhaps one of the most straightforward and easiest ways to get people to *fill in the gaps* is to create a comic strip like the ones found in a newspaper. This does not have to be elaborate, but could simply be stick figures with blank speech and thought bubbles over their heads. Quite literally, the Haverim members would fill in the thoughts or words. The comic strip can then be handed out on a worksheet or displayed on a TV screen. Very simple, but equally effective.

Literature

This may sound simple enough so far, but how do you *d'rash* something that is not a story?

If the passage you want to look at is more of a theological statement, a proclamation, a verse of poetry, or some other form of literature, how do we engage ourselves in it?

The simple answer is by stepping back and creating a 'story' about the passage or an incident based upon it. This week for instance, we *d'rashed* Jesus' words to His disciples:

> *"I no longer call you servants, because a servant does not know his master's business. Instead, I have called you friends, for everything that I learned from my Father I have made known to you."* [66]

We wanted to discover at what point Jesus may have realized His disciples were not simply His colleagues, but those He saw as intimate friends. Also, what implications did that have for us?

The question I presented was:

> If you were Jesus, at what point in the three year discipleship process would you see the disciples or a particular disciple as your friend?

Then I gave them a piece of paper on which to chart Jesus' companionship with the twelve. They plotted what they considered to be key moments in the story of their relationship and presented a graph that showed the peaks and troughs. Near the bottom of the page was a dotted line representing 'servants' and near the top a similar line representing 'friends.' They then reported their findings, including the point at which they felt the relationship broke through to friendship.

For me, it was particularly revealing as I noticed the possibility that Jesus was friends with some of them before they became disciples and that the discipleship paradigm of the day may have affected that relationship. It made me aware of the profound change in relationship when someone I care about joins Pais and becomes a member of my staff. I learned things from my chart about my heart and about God's heart from my friends' charts.

This stepping back can be done with anything and any passage; it just takes a little extra thought.

Piano

The worst use of imagination is to imagine the worst.[67]

I do understand the real fears of this type of engagement in scripture, but the safety net of the *intended* meaning has proven invaluable. It has amazed me how rarely people misinterpret scripture or, more accurately, how when it does happen, the Spirit leads them back. My one piece of advice is based on the art of piano tuning.

When a hundred pianos are tuned, the method used can produce right or wrong results.

If piano number two is tuned to piano number one, and piano three is tuned to piano two, then by the time the one hundredth piano is tuned to piano ninety-nine, it will be significantly out of tune with piano number one. That is the wrong way.

Instead, piano number two is tuned to piano number one, then piano three, thirteen, thirty-three and all others are also tuned to piano number one. This is the correct way.

The *intended* meaning is piano number one.

If the friends who study together are constantly tuning their thoughts, feelings, hopes, and fears to it, then an infinite number of spiritual riffs, tunes, and melodies will complement rather than contradict the conductor of the orchestra.

Even a twelve year old knows that.

Inspired

S'od

Why?

Soil

Wouldn't it be great to become part of the *flow of God's Word*?

> *"Still other seed fell on good soil, where it produced a crop–a hundred, sixty or thirty times what was sown."* [68]

Ever felt that your understanding of God was sown only for you?

Ever felt that your religion was self-absorbed?

Maybe there is a connection.

The good news is that you are a person of peace. When you heard the message of the Kingdom, *you* responded while others did not. When your workmate shared his story of salvation, you requested a further conversation while others walked away. When the preacher gave an altar call, you raised your hand while many stayed motionless. When you read the story of the lost son, you repented while others were unmoved.

The seed fell on your heart, sank deep, and germinated, but it doesn't stop there, does it? The purpose for that seed goes way beyond you, doesn't it?

You know it.

You feel it.

And possibly, it frightens you because it's hard to know what to do next.

With a new revelation comes a new responsibility, but you may find the thought of sharing God's Word difficult. Even though you want the knowledge to be multiplied, you lack the understanding of how to transfer your faith in a complex world with people who need answers that you don't have.

The fourth level of Haverim Devotions™ will encourage us to overcome just that. It creates space for the *contemplation* required to comprehend God's *practices*.

Wouldn't it give you courage to have wise words suddenly drop into your head when you were feeling out of your depth? Wouldn't it feel inspiring to suddenly know things you could not know about yourself or another person that will unlock your heart or theirs? Wouldn't it give you security to step out into the unknown if you knew the unknown was a little more knowable than you thought?

Just as a person of peace should, your peace would pass all understanding.

What?

Contemplation

The fourth level of Haverim Devotions™ is the *inspired* meaning.

The *inspired* meaning reveals the power lying dormant in a passage.

The Hebrew word for this level is *s'od* and it means 'secret.'

The method of the *inspired* meaning is to seek *contemplation*.

More than any other New Testament writer, the Apostle Paul referred to his recognition of the Messiah being God as a revelation of a *s'od*. It is in this *inspired* level that Paul says he found his calling.[69] English Bibles translate the concept of *s'od* as 'mystery.'[70]

If *r'mez* is where scripture interprets scripture, then *s'od* is where the *Spirit* interprets scripture.

Here for the first time, revelation precedes research.

Only when something becomes specific does it become truly dynamic. During our meditations with our Haverim, we can train ourselves to hear God's voice on a passage. Scripture and Spirit combine to bring a dynamism that we may never have previously experienced. We create a place and space where He can speak *to* and *through* us.

If we miss the contemplation, we miss His practices—not because we do not know what God will do, but because we have already decided in advance how He will do it.

When we view a passage from this level, we ask questions such as:

> Lord, what do I not understand about this passage?
>
> What has previously been hidden to me?
>
> What direction do You want to give me?
>
> What specifics do You want to share with me?

Then we wait and listen.

We ask God for a word, key verse, or revelation from the scripture that will be useful to another person in our Haverim. We ask the same questions we have just asked, but for them. Those thoughts we receive can either be written down and passed on paper or spoken aloud to the group.

They can be verbalized or visualized.

The *inspired* level can be the scariest and most challenging to the Haverim, but it has the power to create a defining moment where our lives can change forever.

Wish

Have you ever wished for something?

I have.

So did Moses.

In fact, our wish is exactly the same; I'll explain it in a moment.

I once heard of a preacher who, at the beginning of his sermon, confessed the following:

> "I am so sorry, everybody, but this week I've been busy with funerals and such, so this morning I will just have to rely on the Holy Spirit. Next week however, I promise to be much better prepared."

As humorous as this may be, his Freudian slip allows some us an insight into our own heart and minds.[71] The Holy Spirit is not a dove; He is not a pigeon or a parrot. He is the third person of the Trinity. To be *so* prepared that we are prepared to live life without Him is to cut and never paste God into our lives. We all need to harness His power for the long haul. Just like gasoline, He can simply create a dramatic one-off explosion or be welcomed in to run our spiritual engine. So HD presents the opportunity for more than an event, but rather a constant, ongoing infilling.

You see, the power of the Holy Spirit flows through the whole of the Bible, but we notice a significant difference between His input in the Old Testament and that in the New Testament. Pre-Pentecost, the incidents of the Holy Spirit filling man were occasional and sporadic. He was only poured out for a specific instance, and then He left.

> *Then the Lord came down in the cloud and spoke with him [Moses], and he took some of the power of the Spirit that was on him and put it on the seventy elders. When the Spirit rested on them, they prophesied—but did not do so again.* [72]

Four verses later, Moses wished his wish:

> *"...I wish that all the LORD's people were prophets and that the LORD would put his Spirit on them!"* [73]

Two thousand years later, Moses' request was granted.

On the birthday of the Church, God's Spirit began to be poured out permanently and for all time. But in both cases, the Holy Spirit cannot be stored up. His power must be used at the time of supply so we can be regularly replenished.

I wonder if Moses would have ever imagined a situation like we have today where God *has* poured out His Spirit on all people, but not all of us are taking advantage of Him.

Moses would turn in his grave . . . if he had one.

Washing

When God's message becomes *specific,* it becomes *dynamic.* More than simply encouraging me, it has empowered me.

Here are some ways that this level of HD has shaped my thoughts and life.

One very simple yet profound episode happened a long time before I had any thoughts at all about the Pais Project. As I was reading and praying with friends, one of them turned to me and said:

> "Paul, God has a purpose for you, but it will be like a washing line. A washing line is of no use hung from one pole; it has to be hung between two to do its job."

That short observation, this 'word from God,' meant absolutely nothing to me at the time.

Four years later, I was a solo schools worker in North Manchester finding many young people who wanted to know more about the Gospel. One day, while wondering how to connect them into the wider family of God, I read this passage:

> When he had finished speaking, he said to Simon, "Put out into deep water, and let down the nets for a catch." Simon answered, "Master, we've worked hard all night and haven't caught anything. But because you say so, I will let down the nets." When they had done so, they caught such a large number of fish that their nets began to break. [74]

Or as *The Message* puts it:

> . . . *straining the nets past capacity.* [75]

Immediately the question dropped into my mind:

> *Paul, if you were one of the disciples and you knew a week before that this was going to happen . . . what would you do?*

It was almost a rhetorical question because instantly the answer also hit me:

I would spend the week building the biggest net I could!

Then came the impression . . .

Go do it.

But how?

It was as though God had already given me the understanding four years previously. He had laid the foundation as to how I should apply that passage . . . *partnership.*

A year later, I founded the first Pais Project team, Since then, I have often felt the pressure and expectations of the unique 'washing line' system we had created whereby our apprentices served both a local church and worked for Pais as an organization. Yet this *s'od*, this revelation that preceded the problem, this concept that came from the Spirit not my thinking, has brought me great peace, assuring me we are on the right track. As I reflect twenty years later, I am also reminded that the tension created between serving both a local church and Pais led to the creativity required to reach schools where others had previously failed.

The Spirit *does* wash our brain, not with a desire to wipe its imagination, but with a passion to cleanse it from worldly paradigms.

On many other occasions, I have found that, if I give God the space to speak, He will give me a flow of creativity that I could not or should not realistically expect.

When I am preparing a message, writing a book, or creating a strategy document and have a creative block, I have now learned to stop, take my fingers off the keyboard, and walk up and down my study singing and praising God in the Spirit. I can honestly say that I can only remember one incident in the last few years where that productive void was not filled within a couple minutes, if not seconds, with fresh insight, ideas, and even artistry.

Writer's block is not due to a lack of substance, but a lack of space.

Flower

Many years later, a similar episode to the 'washing line' word happened.

In my book *The Seed and the Cloud*, I unpack the idea of finding God's direction in life.[76] Instead of the typical questions of 'Where should I go? Who should I follow? What should I do?' I propose a different one based on Jesus' words on the mountain:

> *"But seek first his kingdom and his righteousness . . ."*[77]

The question I use to find God's will is:

> What will most advance the Kingdom of God?

When seeking direction, this question rarely lets me down. Sometimes, however, I need some extra help from the Holy Spirit. One major case came when I was leading a church in the UK but was asked to immigrate to the USA in order to create an international base for Pais. This particular day, when asking my usual question, it occurred to me that although I loved both things, the church and Pais, Pais was my *favorite* because it had by far the greatest impact.

I had included the church in my journey from the moment I started to take the request from Texas seriously. Yet I was very surprised when one day, a particularly supportive lady in the church, one who really wanted me to stay, said she felt the Holy Spirit had dropped a message on her heart for me:

> "Paul, the Lord says you must pick your favorite flower and plant it in a place where it would not normally flourish."

The use of the word '*favorite*' was specific, and so the message became dynamic.

The words God gave her for me were probably partly for her as well. It was revelation to her and confirmation to me.

Just as there are many types of *r'mez* and facets of *d'rash*, so there are many variations of *s'od*. The ones I have written about are just a couple of examples. The Spirit may not speak within the actual Haverim meeting; that's not really the point of it. The purpose of our getting together is to prepare us to hear Him while we are chatting with our friends, neighbors, colleagues, and the strangers we meet along the way.

The Spirit plus space equals sharpness.

Axe

There is a story told of a young jobless lumberjack desperate to feed his new family. Approaching a logging company, he begged the foreman for employment but was told no positions were available. The young man was so distressed and concerned about his wife and two small children that, after further pleading, the foreman agreed to give him a four week trial. During it, the hopeful father worked harder than anyone else, and yet at the end of the first week, he was called into the boss' office and fired!

He was told he had started well, but as the week progressed, he had chopped down less and less trees. Stunned and confused, he implored the foreman to give him one more chance, stating that he had worked every moment possible. He explained that he even labored through the morning and lunchtime breaks, still chopping at trees while others rested.

The foreman raised his eyebrows, paused, and asked the lumberjack to give him his axe. Carefully and meticulously, he looked at the workman's only tool, gliding his fingers along the edge of its blade, and then put it down. With a slight smile, he instructed the young man with the following words:

> "I now see the problem. When the other workers take a break, they spend their time not only eating and resting, but sharpening their axes as well. You have not, so your axe is blunt, and that is why you proved such an ineffective employee."

A lesson was learned, and the job offer continued.

The *inspired* level of Haverim Devotions™ will help us sharpen our axes.

How?

Competence

Having a sharp mind is a wonderful gift, but the Spirit does not guarantee to produce one. It is important that the Haverim is trained to not only listen for God's voice, but to discern what is and is not from Him, as well as how to apply what is revealed.

The Spirit and stupidity are a dangerous mix.

Like the man who chose the moment we were both in the gentleman's rest room to tell me, *"Paul, I had a dream about you last night!"* And like the group of young missionaries who, after believing God had given them a message for a disabled man, chased a frightened peg-legged stranger through a carnival screaming at the top of their lungs, *"But we have a message from God for you!"*

"Stupid is as stupid does." [78]

Community builds competence.

The benefit of being part of a Haverim is that it provides a place to practice.

After becoming a Christian in my early teens, I went to a church that trained its members each week in how to hear from God and pass on what you hear. It was probably the most balanced fellowship I have ever had when it comes to *the things of the Spirit.* Believe me, I have seen the extremes of the misuse of 'spiritual gifts' and the denial of them as well.

Perhaps the best advice I was trained to understand might be summed up like this:

> The Spirit will never contradict *His* word . . . or *yours*.

The Holy Spirit will not tell you to do something that goes against the Spirit of the Bible, nor will He encourage you to violate His character within you. It is this kind of wisdom that helps us and this type of accountability that is needed.

The *inspired* level is used to create space for God to make His Word specific to our situation and to that of our friends.

Let us not deny His power, but let us also recognize that revelation comes with boundaries.

Questions

In our Haverim, we have a mixture of people from different backgrounds. Avoiding denominational soundbites and terms has been useful. When it comes to this fourth level, we have not pushed any particular denominational stance. We just create space.

We provide time to contemplate and a purpose for that contemplation.

Within that time, *individual* questions and *friendship* questions are posed.

The *individual* questions are:

> Lord, what do I not yet understand about this passage?
>
> What has been previously hidden to me?
>
> What can't I understand without Your Spirit?
>
> What do You want me to do in response to what I am learning?

Then we ask God for a word, key verse, illustration, or revelation from the scripture that will be useful to another person in our Haverim, the entire group, or someone else in our community.

Our *friendship* questions might be:

> Is there someone else to whom I can pass this message?
>
> How should I do that?

Any thoughts we receive can either be written down and passed on paper or spoken aloud to the group. It is important to remember that the primary objective is not to hear God there and then, although this can of course be a huge benefit. The point is to keep listening for His voice during the rest of our week.

Haverim may not be the moment we receive great answers, but it can be the moment we ask the great questions that lead to us receiving them at another time.

So how can we help people listen for His voice?

Senses

As I have mentioned, one of the benefits of HD is the attraction to post-moderns. A culture that wants to *experience, participate, imagine,* and *connect* is greatly helped when we no longer see Bible study as a one sensory experiment. Good Haverim teachers will take time to think through the setting in which this level is undertaken. Simply dimming lights, lighting candles, and working hard to make sure that distracting noises are limited can greatly enhance the encounter.

Yet, there is more.

Mosaics

> Many years ago, while teaching lessons in public schools, I learned the importance of what we on Pais call 'mosaics,' experiences designed from many fragments. It is true to say that those who advance the Kingdom of God are the ones who go the extra mile, and so rather than turning up five minutes before a class was about to start, our habit was to arrive much earlier to recreate the room with permission from the teacher. We found that familiarity is an enemy of faith,

and that even by moving the chairs and tables around to create a different setting, we created anticipation. A sense that something was about to happen hung in the air, and in my opinion, stirring anticipation is the first step to encouraging the faith needed to expect something new.

A Haverim teacher will do well to copy the idea that we had, which was to involve as many of the senses as we could. One of the first times we did this was on a lesson about forgiveness. Wanting to emphasize the negative impact of bitterness, we went to town to create a mosaic experience. As the students walked, the song *Don't Look Back in Anger* by Oasis was playing, and we had games where students would bite into particularly sour citrus fruit. We used smell, sight, sound, and touch to help them get the message.

I am in no way saying that at the fourth stage of HD we need to create a Broadway theater production; I'm simply encouraging you to put a little extra thought into creating expectations of the Spirit and involving the senses in our contemplation.

Sights

When we start our contemplations, I sometimes use visual aids as a catalyst. This is a delicate and finely balanced skill because we want participants to focus on the passage or verse, not the image in front of them. The images should not take away from the passage, but form a backdrop to help focus prayer and intercession. The point of these exercises is not to bring revelation from these images, but for these images to help bring revelation from the passage.

Many years ago, a lady gave a Pais director a copy of the famous black and white photo of construction workers sitting on a beam of an unfinished New York City skyscraper. Do you know the one I mean? In the picture, the men casually eat their packed lunches while sitting perched on an iron girder with their legs dangling high above the New York bustle.[79] She told my friend that this photo had spoken to her of the Pais leadership. They inspired her by living at such a height of faith, believing God for their provision, and yet seeming so relaxed. She said this gave her faith to believe God for her provision as well. I have used this photo to help people contemplate the parable of the talents:

To those who use well what they are given, even more will be given, and they will have an abundance. [80]

I show the photo and then pose the following question:

> What might God want of you that is a natural gift of yours but could be done to such a height of faith that it inspires others to be courageous?

I have used video clips in this manner as well. Remember, the key is that the visual aid becomes no more than a catalyst to the passage of scripture being contemplated.

Sound

We all know that music is a great aid to meditation. Besides blocking out other noises that can become a distraction, music inspires. Sometimes God uses music where teaching has failed. How many times have you seen someone caught up in worship to such an extent that they make a commitment to something they would not normally, rationally do? Why do so many men use background music to make their move and offer a proposal of marriage?

The Holy Spirit also uses sounds and melodies to pull our hearts in a direction that our minds stubbornly refuse to go.

A key to using music at the *inspired* level is to play something that does not have words. Instead, it should be chosen for its mood or emotional qualities—it may be stirring, it may be sad, it may be robust, it may be gentle. If you play a worship song, then the likelihood is that people's hearts and minds won't be tuned into the Holy Spirit, but tuned into the words of its composer.

Taste

Perhaps even the type of meal eaten when your Haverim gathers can spark revelation in the hearts of your group. God has used this sense many times throughout history, putting into place certain meals and feasts. He has led His people to specific types of food in order to not simply remind them of what has happened, but to connect them to a deeper level of the story. At times in Israel, people literally tasted their *Torah*.

Perhaps a creative Haverim host can participate in this level by occasionally prescribing a meal that acts as a stimulus to intercession.

Smell

History tells us that the Church often used incense and smells to send a message. When Jesus appeared before Pilate, His body had been infused with expensive perfume. He literally smelt of His death to come. When He stood before king and governor, although He said little with His lips, His body revealed through fragrance that His trials were a farce. What must God have revealed to His accusers simply by the smell of Jesus?

Just like music, we've all experienced how a sudden smell has taken us back to another time and place. Perhaps this sense can be creatively engaged in our Bible study.

Speech

I often find it helpful to keep a meditation exercise flowing by occasionally speaking simple words and phrases into the mix. As people are meditating on God and how He interacts with us, one idea is to occasionally throw into the mix one of the names of God. Invoking 'Jehovah,' 'Abba,' 'El Shaddai,' 'Elohim,' and other such descriptions not only provide food for thought, but also a catalyst for meditation. Long silences are sometimes best punctuated with words that keep people on track.

Touch

> Objects don't have to be seen to help us believe. In one Haverim group a few months ago, an object was passed around veiled by a thin piece of cloth. The friends had to guess its identity. They then reflected on what it felt like to hold a truth in your hands but see it *dimly* through a veil.

> Even touch can be used as a catalyst if the right questions are posed by the Haverim teacher.

Einstein

Questions, creativity, and community: all vital ingredients in the pursuit of Godly wisdom.

Even Einstein conducted what he called 'thought experiments.' I would have expected him to do incredible amounts of research and calculations, and then deduce his theories. Instead, he daydreamed. Occasionally he would be inspired, and then he researched to see if his revelation was correct. This was how he came up with the theories of general relativity and special relativity—by looking out his window or imagining a man falling off a roof in an elevator.

Now remember, he needed to know the basics of science first—the *p'shat*, if you like.

However, one Pais director pointed out that it may be better on occasion to put *s'od* first in our study of a passage. As the *inspired* level is last, it is sometimes weakened due the fact that minds are no longer virgin territory and have now been filled with the thoughts and ideas of everyone's interpretations.

So on occasion, moving the levels around may not only be productive, but may also free us from a regimented approach to HD.

U2

With that in mind, let me encourage you with one final observation.

The lead singer of U2, the most famous band on the planet, sang:

> "I have spoken with the tongues of angels [. . .] but I still haven't found what I'm looking for." [81]

The key to being constantly filled with the Spirit is to know why you were looking for it in the first place. If you are searching to understand the secrets of His purpose and to carry with you His presence, then you are searching for the right reasons.

Or, as one rabbi said:

> ". . . we walk around in pursuit of *p'shat* and afraid of *s'od*, thinking that we know all we must to make life work as it should, and then wonder why it doesn't. It is *s'od* that is closest to G-d in the hierarchy of learning, and though you can't soar in the clouds until you learn to first walk on earth, you must learn to walk on the earth with the goal to one day soar in the clouds." [82]

We must stop *trying* and start *training*.

INFRASTRUCTURE

Who?

Everyone

Everyone. That is who Haverim is for. The whole purpose of this method of teaching is that it is easily and quickly transferable.

It is *inclusive* rather than *exclusive*.

In a Haverim, the role of the teacher is to facilitate rather than instruct. My hope and desire is that the four levels of the Haverim Devotions™ will become something you can do with someone of no faith, little faith, or another faith.

Party!

Over the past couple of years, it has been my pleasure to get to know Jonny and Vanessa, a young married couple who eagerly desire to share with their neighbors the faith they are excited about. Both are heavily involved in their local church activities, yet uncommonly, they still make time to touch the lives of those not a part of a church. Jonny works in his local Starbucks as a barista, and every one of his colleagues has visited his Haverim. Several are now part of it.

Jonny shares their story below:

> "Vanessa and I started out with parties. We love to throw parties. Ever since we arrived in St. Louis, we have hosted parties for friends to come and hang out and meet other people. This spectrum of people is quite broad—people we met that day all the way to our very own

families. The reason we do this is because we love to celebrate all the different cultures that make up our community of friends. It doesn't matter what faith or background you have, it's all about coming and being served good food and drink and getting to know people of a beautiful culture and ethnicity.

"This has really provided opportunities for us to begin a conversation with our community about the journey of faith we are all on. HD helps us do this as it opens up deep conversations. People can bring their journeys and experiences to the table without having to push them through a Christian filter. Pain, frustration, confusion about who God is—these are things we all experience, and this brings us together as people on the journey of faith.

"Haverim Devotions™ provides a tool that Christians, atheists, agnostics, Muslims, Jews, and every other religion and worldview can use to express their ideas and go deeper into learning who the one true God is.

"To us, it really has been about becoming a family. No matter what differences of opinion we have or what different faiths we have, we love each other and see one another as our very own. We do simple things together, like eating meals. We do this at least once a week and share our stories around some good food.

"We also serve together. One day of every month, we seek to fulfill our community's biggest need. So Haverim to me is a place of peace, friendship, love, and faith all lived out as a family together."

Sounds a little too good to be true doesn't it?

But it's not. Neither is it 'smash and grab' evangelism.

It is invested and intentional friendship.

There is an argument, isn't there? Its two extremes might be labeled 'conquest' and 'cowardice.' One says tell people the gospel and don't hold back;

the other says make friends with no strings attached. Neither is altogether Biblical.

The kind of friendship that Jonny and Vanessa describe *is* one with no strings attached. They are not puppets playing the part of friends while preparing to be pulled out of people's lives the minute they don't respond to the puppeteer. Yet friendship, real friendship, will always want the best for their friends. It will always be intentional. What is flowing out of this couple is not a presentation, but a natural overflow of their hearts. They are attached to the Father, and so they can have a natural friendship that does not have to rely on a program.

However, another reason to doubt their story remains. Will those *not* professing Christ as their savior really want to engage in the Word of God?

Yes . . . if they are given space to share their own thoughts.

Yes . . . if they are given the Spirit as their primary teacher.

Yes . . . if they are given the right to be wrong . . . and the right to be right.

Keys

So how do those not following Jesus authentically benefit from the four levels? How might it be adapted in a work place at lunchtime or in a home, pub, or Starbucks? Here are some thoughts based on feedback from Jonny, Vanessa, and others.

Intended

> Perhaps most surprising is the positive reaction to the *intended* meaning, the *p'shat*.
>
> Non-Christians get to see the historical context that lies behind what we are studying. In doing so, they begin to realize that the Bible isn't just a bunch of stories hanging in a vacuum of fantasy. When people see archaeology, history, and literature outside of the Bible connecting with the stories, prophecies, and history within it, credibility is given to its contents.

Depending on your group, you may want to encourage people to bring any research books they wish to this level of study. For instance, material explaining the history, customs, or practices of the period you are looking at does not have to be the kind of book you find in a religious store. If it is not seen as a Christian book, yet provides context and couples well with the Bible passage, then perhaps this is even more powerful!

Implied

For *r'mez*, they experience the fluidity of the scriptures and how things correlate. Specifically, they get to see how the Messianic psalms and prophecies work together and how scripture helps interpret itself and future things.

For both the *intended* and *implied* levels, consider how you can help those who may be less literate than yourself. The level of academia can be simply determined by the kind of material you give them to research. For instance, I recently advised a Pais team working with a group of young people with low education not to give out books, but instead to create a fact sheet. I suggested it could be a mixture of simple facts in both word and picture format.

Love finds a way.

Interpreted

D'rash goes down great with those not yet following Christ because as Jonny pointed out, *"People like to tell their own story."* They like to express themselves in a particular situation that has already happened, and it helps them to discover and chat through their own motives. *D'rash* helps people relate to a book they never thought they could relate to!

Ultimately our friends can come to terms with why the characters in the stories did what they did—even if that character is or represents God. They begin to associate and feel for the scripture they are reading as they become emotionally and mentally involved.

Inspired

> *S'od* is an interesting one with non-believers.
>
> How can the Spirit speak to those He does not live within?
>
> You might be surprised. The impact of someone praying for you is, as someone mentioned last night in the Haverim on our street, "a bonding experience."
>
> Coming into a safe environment to be quiet, reflect, and meditate while others do the work can be very enticing to some, especially if they suddenly feel connected to the people of God in a way they may never have felt before.

You may be reading this thinking, *I just can't see it*

Well, if you are imagining strangers, you would be right. Most of the levels might not affect someone who is not interested in God and not seeking answers.

Imagine instead those of no faith, little faith, or another faith, but wanting faith. Think of people you have made authentic friendships with, people who have not been press-ganged into attending but are curious.

Jesus said *spread* the message of the Kingdom, *spot* the people of peace, *stay* with them, and then *send* them out to those who previously rejected Him.[83] With such people, Haverim works.

Love

Haverim has one essential ingredient: *Love.*

It is love for people and love for God in the heart of a Christian that will drive us to encourage our neighbor, colleague, or friend to join us in our journey of faith.

Expertise in handling God's Word, although an obvious benefit, is not essential. An academic mind, although helpful on some levels, is not necessary. A long-standing relationship with God, although bringing maturity, is in no way a requirement.

But *love* is.

I learned a vital lesson years ago during my work in schools. A week after I became a Christian, God healed me of a skin disease, and I would often tell the story in schools with very different results. I presented a mixture of lessons and assemblies, as well as weekly lunch clubs. The lunch clubs had a different dynamic because they were attended each week by the same young people and so, after a few months, a relationship would be built, and in some small way, we would become friends.

When I told my healing story in an assembly or lesson, it had a mild impact. Some were curious, but many simply dismissed it because I was a stranger telling them something very strange.

In the lunch club, however, a peculiarly different reaction occurred. You see, it is easy to dismiss the crazy story of a stranger you don't know. Yet it is difficult to dismiss the same story when someone you trust tells you something your secular upbringing has repeatedly informed you is impossible. The faces of those non-believing young people of peace revealed shock and awe. I remember one particular student vocalizing his inner torment.

"But that can't be!" he shouted out. "But I believe you! But . . . ah, my head hurts!"

Haverim means *friends* who study together, not strangers who go to church together. This unique form of Bible discovery is not created by a controlled environment, but a culture of people who love God and the things God loves: *People.*

How?

Two

Just let me reiterate, in case you are confused.

This idea of Haverim has two parts: Haverim and Haverim Devotions™.

Haverim is the community group whose primary intention is to know God and make Him known in their neighborhood; some describe them as *missional communities*. Haverim Devotions™ is the tool, the method of study in which they employ the four levels. This method is used within the Haverim, but can also be used separately from it.

HD should be your *servant*; you should not become its *slave*.

You could use one or all of the four levels outside of a Haverim group as long as you have a plan, a strategy whereby you are hoping to make friends with whom you can go on a journey of faith. I pray that the Haverim Devotions™ or any part of them never become a gimmick or a fun way to add a bit of spice to a traditional Bible study.

D'rash was never intended to simply grow a church Bible study.

Subject

Because the fundamental point of a Haverim is to teach people *how* to think not *what* to think, and our ambition is to touch the lives of all, the subject matter is best determined by those in the group.

One of the vital dynamics that helped me get Pais teams into schools that had rejected other organizations, especially churches, was our different approach. We never offered a pre-programmed package, carefully manicured with a bow on it. Instead, we offered role-models who could prepare a presentation on anything the school wanted as long as it was based on common values. This is also a benefit of Haverim and Haverim Devotions™. The study can be done in response to the needs of those attending rather than deciding in advance what we think they might want or need to hear. This in itself is more attractive.

The Haverim may want to look at a certain difficult subject, a question of theology they have often struggled with, or a fascinating story. Your workmates, however, may wish to tackle something topical that has raised issues in their lives. They know you are a Christian and now, facing a particular situation, they may need someone to help them navigate and understand what they are going through.

You must be flexible.

You can use the full four levels of HD or introduce your friend to it with a lunchtime conversation where you simply get them to *d'rash* a story. The story could be a passage about the thing they are going through, perhaps a parable. The story might not even be a Biblical one. Instead, it might be a story you made up that contains a truth about the Kingdom, or you might give them a Biblical story set in a modern day era.

The key is to get them engaged and give yourself and the Spirit a chance to speak to them.

Cycle

Haverim is more than a Bible study.

It is a place where we train to understand, but also reach out into our neighborhoods. So how do we fit these two things in? Well, that is for you to decide, but please allow me to make one possible suggestion. Recently, I have noticed that some Haverim groups have found the following monthly cycle a natural fit. This was not always intentional and it is not the only possibility; it just seems to work.

A typical four week month is split in the following way:

> The first week, the *intended* and *implied* levels of study are examined. Both levels naturally fit together because they are research-based. The second week, the *interpreted* level of study is experienced. The third week, the *inspired* level of study is explored.

> This provides three separate meetings of the Haverim studying the same scripture from three very different angles. In our group, we meet for two hours. The first half hour we eat, the next hour we study, and the final half hour we relax together. This works well for us since we have parents who bring small children, but something different might work better for you.

> The fourth week is an occasion to make friends with the community. This can happen many different ways and is best determined by the members of the Haverim and the community in which it is set.

In St. Louis, Jonny and Vanessa's Haverim has a mixture of ethnicity, so house parties with a different cultural theme such as Hispanic or German work great for every fourth week. They have held African, English, and Asian parties with food and games from those regions. Texas lends itself to cookouts, and so we put the grill on the *front* driveway and invite the neighbors. We have face-painting for the children and a slip'n'slide. We put out chairs and invite neighbors to chat and play lawn games. We pass out flyers to the connecting streets each month, but we don't give a label to our group. We just announce neighborhood parties or events.

Over the last few months, this simple activity has earned very positive comments from our neighbors. A typical statement is: "We have often said our community needs something like this, but we never knew how to start it or what to do."

What you do is immaterial; how you do it is more important. For it to work, you need followers of Christ who are keen to advance the Kingdom of God.

They have to want to make friends, because this is more than simply inviting people to a meeting. They have to resist the temptation to launch into their testimony with everyone they meet; instead they must learn how to journey with people first.[84]

Apart from community *recreational* events, the fourth week can also provide an opportunity for community *service* projects where the Haverim offers practical support to an individual or partners with a neighborhood project. This again provides an opportunity for the Haverim to be a catalyst in the community, offering a chance for those people of peace who are service-oriented in their personality to get involved and journey with you.

Haverim, you see, is a tool for discipleship.

Leaders

Again, the way you set up the leadership of your home-based Haverim is up to you. We split it into three roles rather than put all the responsibility on one person or couple which has proven difficult for other small group formats. The three duties are as follows:

> The Haverim *leader* is responsible to oversee the group. They determine the recreational events and organize the people. They oversee the logistics and encourage us to keep on track with the vision.

> The Haverim *teacher* is responsible for the studies. They determine the passages of scripture with the group and lead many of the studies, but also train others within the group to teach as well.

> The Haverim *host* houses the Haverim if it meets in a home. They offer their hospitality and coordinate the food. They tidy the house and set it up for the meeting.

A typical Haverim meeting does need some coordination, and having appointed leaders helps.

Church

I believe in Church.

I believe in big churches.

I believe in big, lively, well-done churches.

I personally don't believe that church should only be done in homes, the golf club, the pub, or some other small setting. I don't have a problem if you do; I just think that Haverim is best done in the context of something bigger than itself.

As before, these are just my suggestions on how you might operate your Haverim within a bigger picture. It's just an idea.

It seems to me that the early Church got some things right. Certainly not everything, but one thing that naturally happened was that it morphed itself into the usual anthropologically sound structure of three levels of connection. They met together as a large gathering in the temple courts, they met together in regional groups, and they met in homes.

Big. Medium. Small.

It seems that most of the world's societies do this, probably because each of these gathering sizes provides opportunity for a distinctive type of connection.

If I ever lead a church again, this might be my approach:

> The big setting, where everyone would come together once a week. This would provide the *motivation* for our *mission*. The big setting offers the opportunity for all the spiritual gifts of the church to come together and, with the aid of synergy, do something with excellence that benefits the entire fellowship of the saints.

> The medium setting, where everyone in a region would meet on some regular basis. This would provide the *implementation* of the *mission*. Big church tends to draw people from far and wide and, in

doing so, has less concentrated influence in one geographical area. Meeting as a medium-sized group can encourage people to own the vision for their part of the city or region. These meetings would not have a sermon, but a celebration. It would be the time to tell local stories of what God is doing; it would be a time to recruit, and from it would come regional projects.

The small setting, where everyone in a local neighborhood would meet once a week. This would provide the *nurturing* of the people on *mission*. It offers the opportunity for people to train and be discipled along the way. It provides a place for them to share how they are using HD in their school, street, or workplace and to be encouraged and advised on how to do it even better.

Haverim is ideal as a small setting program.

On occasion, the church building might be the best place to *teach* new leaders of a Haverim its concepts and strategy. Perhaps courses could be set up to give instructions on how to draw a Haverim together and how to develop the generic skills and characteristics of a leader.

The only place to *train* people in Haverim Devotions™, however, is in a Haverim itself.

Kevin

As a leader, I have a particular burden to equip other leaders with hearts similar to mine.

When I first started working in schools almost twenty-five years ago, Kevin was a mentor to me and God's resource for my work in many different ways. For a long time we lost touch, but I discovered that we had both moved to the States. I was here setting up an international base for Pais, while he had been involved in extremely large churches in the North. Although we were on different journeys as far as the pragmatics of our work, when we reconnected, we realized our spiritual journeys were almost parallel.

Since he and his family planted a church, they decided to launch a Haverim group. Finding that the practice fulfilled much of the theory, within the next few months, they launched three more and are planning to establish more Haverim groups throughout their city.

I will let Kevin explain why:

"Over the last ten years I had become increasingly concerned about the lack of passion amongst church members for evangelism. I wondered out loud to many of my fellow leaders and we discussed mission, discipleship, and the general lack of desire for God's Word that I had observed. I wondered if there was a link. Perhaps the deficit of God's Word in the hearts of our people leads to less desire to be discipled and share their faith.

"I was also concerned for other pastors who felt my desire to see their local church grow and be involved in making disciples. I, like many other leaders, wondered how we could change communities, nevermind fill our church buildings.

"Then in 2010 I reconnected with my old friend Paul Gibbs and began to learn about Haverim Devotions™ from him. I started to practice this form of Bible study with my wife and sometimes close family members. We discovered its impact on our lives and saw this as a fresh and different idea that might produce fresh and different results.

"When we eventually launched Saints Church, we began meeting with a group of people and became 'Friends in Study Together.' Utilizing social media in between our weekly Haverim meetings, we approached the Book of Acts together and a fresh picture of a missional church began to appear.

"Our desire was for missional communities rather than support groups or interest groups, and Haverim has helped us with that tremendously. The most beneficial part of its DNA is the renewed passion it brings to people's lives and with that, a renewed desire for community rather than just the Sunday experience. We are discovering that people are more excited about mission and also are beginning to desire and participate in discipleship and mentoring within the community. We have seen both established believers and those who would never normally visit a church participate together due to its peculiar format; both are able to make important contributions.

"There is no spiritual class system."

I asked Kevin why he thought HD works with people with no faith, little faith, or another faith. This was his reply:

"It does work with non-believers, but you have to make friends with them first. Once we have earned their trust, we hang out, have coffee, barbecue, and meet their families. We explain to them what we do and that we meet in groups.

"The first question is, 'Is this like regular church where they stand at a pulpit and tell us how to believe?' No, we tell them, it is a journey, an explanation of what we have learned as a group. We do things that friends do together.

"We tell them it is not simply about your questions, it is about our questions together. We rarely end up answering traditional questions about whether there were dinosaurs on the ark but deeper questions.

"How the two mix is another conversation. One night we had the seasoned Christians on the couch across the room from three totally unchurched and unsaved people. One leaned forward and asked, 'When were you born of the blood?' The non-believers were confused. So, we make friends first and later invite them to the study."

I think this last point is key.

Joel

My eldest son is a talker. It gets him into trouble, especially when he was in school. One day a substitute teacher, fed up with his chatter, finally decided to send him to the principal's office with the words:

> *"You're very good at a fake British accent, but please stop it!"*

It took his classmates some time to rescue him from punishment by convincing her that he was in fact English. When she realized, she apologized.

She did not understand him because she did not know him.

Calling

What is the role of Christian leadership? What were you called to do by Jesus when you were appointed to lead God's people? Some of us might think that what Kevin describes sounds good and well, but we are unsure if our people could pull it off. We perhaps doubt that our congregations would be able to make friends and communicate their faith in this way.

Well, whose fault is that?

Is it really that they cannot or that our church culture denies them the strategy and opportunity to make friends? Is it because, unlike Jesus' teaching, our sermons don't require them to? Or maybe our sermons do, but our strategies don't? Do we train people how to make friends or simply how to reiterate our sermons?

Maybe Jesus' brother was right . . .

> *You do not have, because you do not ask . . .*[85]

Perhaps we don't ask our congregation, and so we don't ask God. I don't mean for this to be harsh or condemning, I simply intend to stir our hearts, minds, and emotions. So let me ask you a question instead:

> What were you called to do?

> And *when* were you called to start doing it?

When?

Asthma

I wonder if you remember the first time you ever asked a question about the Church.

My first time was in the middle of an asthma attack.

Twenty-five years ago, I was running through the streets of Glasgow with cramp in my stomach and spasms in my chest. I had been racing to intercept the coach that would take me home to a mission center where I was based. Missing it meant I would be homeless for the night.

I had just taken part in a street theater production where I played 'man.' It was a powerfully designed mime that took people from creation to the resurrection in less than ten minutes. Our belief was simple: we were going to change the world and it was going to start on the streets of Scotland. On this particular day after we performed on the street, I shared my personal journey of faith and a young man approached me to ask questions. He wanted to find out more about my faith and, importantly, how it could be his. After listening to him, I led him through the 'sinner's prayer,' then I immediately turned to the leader of the mission and asked:

"What do we do now?"

I wondered how I was supposed to plug him into a local church. What was the plan to help him on his way towards growing and developing into someone who could pursue the Kingdom for himself?

My mission leader simply replied:

> "Nothing. We've done our job."

Instinctively, I knew this was wrong. So I asked permission to take him to the nearest congregation. Permission was granted, but came with a warning:

> "You had better be quick; dinner is waiting for us and the coach leaves in twenty minutes with or without you."

Briskly we walked through the streets, and when I found a church, I knocked on its door. Over the next few minutes, I connected this new member of the Kingdom with the minister who answered. Running back to the place where we had performed, I found that the team had departed. And so my marathon began, a desperate and frantic race through the inner city to intercept my ride home.

Moments before I jumped into the middle of the road putting both hands up, playing a near fatal game of 'chicken' with the coach driver, the question racing through my mind had been . . .

> *Do we really believe this is going to happen?*

Every day during my four-month training course, we had prayed for revival in Scotland, and yet I wondered if our lack of strategy suggested that deep down we never really believed it would work.

Traffic

This very same question has haunted me for the last twenty-five years.

It has led me to establish the Pais Project, now working in public schools on five continents. It has nagged me, provoked me, and spurred me on. It has empowered me, equipped me, and encouraged me to connect with many others who have their own version of the same question.

Recently, it has even encouraged Pais to create the Pais Collective and the Pais Venture, the vision being to provide a way for both churches and businesses to think through that question in three different areas of life: *mission*, *discipleship*, and *study*.

This book is about one of those areas: *study*. Two future books in this trilogy will look at mission and discipleship. Neither will be written to simply pose questions and pull down what went before. Instead, all three are intended to build on what has gone before and suggest a way forward.

Why?

Well, I have lived in a city called Arlington, Texas, for seven years now. It has well over 300,000 residents and lies in the middle of the metroplex, a conglomeration of many other cities including Dallas, Fort Worth, and, north of us, two of the fastest growing cities in America. I have two local airports; the largest is said to be bigger than Manhattan Island! Yet, since we emigrated from England, I have been in a major traffic jam only a handful of times. Some may say I just need to get out more. Possibly true, but I think there may be another reason.

Texas was built with the car in mind.

In England, our ancient cities were established before the production car was a twinkling in Henry Ford's eye. Back home, the roads are narrow, winding, and squeeze themselves into the small spaces remaining after hundreds of years of industrial development. Yet in Texas, visionary genius lies behind the way its road systems were designed. Huge, wide-open highways were cut through the state before the need for many of them had arisen.

When it comes to *mission*, *discipleship*, and *study*, our words reveal that these things are in our hearts, but do our programs and strategies betray the fact that they are not truly in our thinking?

We are growing crowds, but are we empowering communities?

I know many successful pastors who look at their congregations, wondering if their people are that much different than those outside the church walls. A few are trying to change things by bringing new challenges, but some that are doing so are now losing churchgoers.

As one author implied, we advertise Christianity like a luxury liner, but when people walk up the gangplank they realize it is a battleship and promptly walk off.[86] Bait and switch does not work in the Kingdom of God.

Artificial rewards produce artificial results.

So let me pass my thorn in the flesh onto you . . .

When will we all agree that we need large attractive churches, but designed from the foundation up with an approach to the Word of God that we honestly believe will work?

When will we create, promote, and teach a form of Bible study that can be passed on by the average Christian to their neighbor? When will we even see that as important?

When will we commit to an approach to the scriptures that encourages the saints to commit to understanding the *heart* of God, not just His rules and rewards?

When will we redesign our programs to produce the kind of people who want to participate in the kind of mission Jesus had in mind?

When will we be able to truly believe in what we do?

INFORMATION

Where?

Glance

Are you confused? Is this all too much? Are you unsure how the different levels fit together? Have you noted that there are 'I' words, 'C' words, 'P' words, and Hebrew words that are supposed to connect in some kind of way, but you are not sure how?

Let me suggest that you go to the website www.haverimdevotions.com where you can see the 'Haverim Devotions: At a Glance' chart. It allows you to take a step back and see how everything joins together.

Thanks again for reading the book. I really hope it helps you discover new truths and understand God's heart a bit more fully.

Paul

Endnotes

1. Thomas Jefferson [italics added].

2. The English comedian Peter Kay once pointed out that no matter how long Shaggy and Scooby ran, the scenery behind them seemed to be on a loop.

3. Brian Stelter, "Youths Are Watching, but Less Often on TV." *New York Times Online*, February 8, 2012. http://www.nytimes.com/2012/02/09/business/media/young-people-are-watching-but-less-often-on-tv.html?pagewanted=all&_r=0.

4. Hebrews 5:12.

5. Leonard Sweet, *Post-Modern Pilgrims: First Century Passion for the 21st Century World* (Nashville: Boardman & Holman Publishers, 2000).

6. William H. Gates III, *Business @ the Speed of Thought: Succeeding in the Digital Economy* (London: Penguin Group, 1999).

7. I am referencing Max Lucado, Bill Hybels, Rick Warren, and Francis Chan. They are all great writers whom I respect, therefore this comment is not a reflection on them, but upon those of us who read them.

8. CNN. (2011) *Interview with James Dyson*. Interviewed by Fareed Zakara [TV] November 27, 2011.

9. 'Perverted' being best understood as something deviating from its original purpose.

10. The late Margaret Thatcher said this during what was coined by the Scottish press as the "Sermon on the Mound," her address to the General Assembly of the Church of Scotland, May 21, 1988.

11. Paul Clayton Gibbs, *The Cloud and the Line* (Arlington, TX: Harris House Publishing, 2011).

12. The cloud references are in Exodus 13:21, 14:24, 16:10, 19:9; Numbers 9:15; Matt. 17:5, 24:30; and Rev. 14:14.

13. Between 530 BC and AD 70 when the Second Temple of Jerusalem was in place and in which the Gospels and most of the book of Acts took place.

14. David H. Stern, *Jewish New Testament Commentary* (Clarksville, MD: Jewish New Testament Publications, Inc., 1992), 11-12.

15. Matthew 13:3-23.

16. The *mishnah* is an authoritative collection of exegetical material embodying the oral tradition of Jewish law and forming the first part of the Talmud.

17. Brad Young, *The Parables: Jewish Tradition and Christian Interpretation* (Peabody, MA: Hendrickson Publishers, 1998), 266.

18. Matthew 13:23.

19. Babylonian Talmud Hagigah 14b; Jerusalem Talmud Hagigah 2:1.

20. Matthew 13:4.

21. Torah is defined as "the body of wisdom and law contained in Jewish Scripture and other sacred literature and oral tradition" and "the five books of Moses constituting the Pentateuch." Merriam Webster, s.v. "Torah," accessed April 23, 2013, http://www.merriam-webster.com/dictionary/torah.

22. Dr. Ron Moseley, *Yeshua: A Guide to the Real Jesus and the Original Church* (Clarksville,MD: Messianic Jewish Publishers, 1996), 126-7.

23. John 3:5.

24. John 11:17.

25. David H. Stern, *Jewish New Testament Commentary* (Clarksville, MD: Jewish New Testament Publications, Inc., 1992), 189-190.

26. Jesus raised the widow's son at Nain in Luke 7:11-17 and Jairus' daughter in Matthew 9:18-26.

27. Acts 15:28-29.

28. The Noahide laws are recognized as traditional ethical values (*The Jewish New Testament Commentary*, 278). During the 102nd Congress of the United States of America, March 5, 1991, they were referenced as the ethical values and principles at the bedrock of society. *Tosefta* refers to the collection of traditions in the Jewish oral law (*Jewish Encyclopedia*, http://www.jewishencyclopedia.com/articles/14458-tosefta). *Talmud* here is a generic designation for an entire body of Jewish literature which includes writings of Jewish tradition (*Jewish Encyclopedia*, http://www.jewishencyclopedia.com/articles/14213-talmud).

29. This is the more typical phrase that is used by rabbis based on scriptures such as Talmud Shabbat 63a when Rabbi Kahana objected to Mar son of Rabbi Huna: "*A verse cannot depart from its plain meaning.*"

30. Matthew 11:3.

31. Share your ideas on the website haverimdevotions.com where you can find pools of helpful suggestions and resources.

32. In the past, I have used books such as *Freemans Manners and Customs of the Bible*, *In Search of Paul*, or *The Parables* by Brad Young.

33. Two I have used in the past are *Baker Encyclopedia of Christian Apologetics* and *Hard Sayings of the Bible*, but many others are available.

34. Brad Young, *The Parables: Jewish Tradition and Christian Interpretation* (Peabody, MA: Hendrickson Publishers, 1998).

35. Matthew 13:5-6.

36. *NIV Life Application Study Bible* (Grand Rapids: Zondervan & Wheaton, Tyndale House Publishers, Inc. 1984). Note on Matthew 13:2-3.

37. Matthew 27:46.

38. Psalm 22:14-18.

39. Psalm 22:23-24; 27; 29-31.

40. Matthew 11:3.

41. Matthew 11:4-5.

42. Matthew 11:6.

43. Mark 5:25-29.

44. Malachi 4:2.

45. Anne Spangler and Lois Tverberg, *Sitting at the Feet of Rabbi Jesus: How the Jewishness of Jesus Can Transform Your Faith* (Grand Rapids: Zondervan, 2009), 246.

46. I have Pastor Harry Letson, one of my spiritual mentors, to thank for this, as he pointed this out to me many years ago.

47. Luke 22:42. Story also in Matthew 26.

48. Zechariah 14:4-5.

49. Matthew 26:31 quoting Zechariah 13:7.

50. Matthew 13:7.

51. Matthew 13:52.

52. All of the sages said this, but it is stated in 'Bamidbar Rabba 13:15,' which is a Jewish document, a *midrash* from classical Judaism.

53. *Midrash* is the name for a certain type of interpretation, a collection of them, or the exercise of creating them.

54. 2 Kings 13:14-19.

55. 2 Kings 13:14b.

56. After studying context for a while, you will begin to store away all sorts of information that becomes applicable to many different scriptures. This was the case here. Although I cannot remember exactly where I originally learned this tidbit; I believe it was from Jack Hayford, *The Hayford Bible Handbook* (Nashville: Thomas Nelson, Inc., 1995).

57. Matthew 16:18.

58. 2 Kings 13:18-19.

59. Matthew 14:22-27.

60. A study of God, not a study of people.

61. Genesis 32:24.

62. Tag-team is an activity where the participants take turns participating as team members.

63. You can check out the old youtube video at: http://youtu.be/5F18Vcxgl1U.

64. Arabian proverb.

65. Ideally, this is a restating of things already discovered by the Haverim during the previous two levels but they can also be brought by the Haverim leader.

66. John 15:15.

67. You can find more thoughts on this and imagination's impact on vision from my book *The Line and the Dot* (Arlington, TX: Harris House Publishing, 2010).

68. Matthew 13:8.

69. Galatians 1:11-16.

70. These are two scriptures that attest to this: Colossians 2:2-3: ("...in order that they may know the mystery [s'od] of God, namely, Christ [Messiah], in whom is hidden all the treasures of wisdom & knowledge") and 1 Corinthians 2.7 ("...we declare God's wisdom, a mystery [s'od]that has been hidden and that God destined for our glory before time began").

71. A Freudian slip is a par praxis whereby we inadvertently say something that deep down we really think or mean.

72. Numbers 11:25.

73. Numbers 11:29.

74. Luke 5:4-6.

75. Luke 5:6 (*The Message*).

76. This book, not yet released, is the third in the Kingdom Trilogy, which consists of *The Line and the Dot: The Kingdom Pioneers* (2010), *The Cloud and the Line: The Kingdom Principles* (2011), and *The Seed and the Cloud: The Kingdom Patterns* (publication date pending as of this writing).

77. Matthew 6:33.

78. Forrest Gump's mother in *Forrest Gump,* directed by Robert Zemeckis (Hollywood, CA: Paramount Home Entertainment, 1994), DVD.

79. To view the photo I'm describing, 'Lunch atop a Skyscraper *(New York Construction Workers Lunching on a Crossbeam),*' go to weblink: http://en.wikipedia.org/wiki/Lunch_atop_a_Skyscraper.

80. Matthew 25:29 (New Living Translation, 2007).

81. U2 and Bono (1987), "Still Haven't Found What I'm Looking For." On *The Joshua Tree* [CD]. Dublin: Island (1986).

82. Rabbi Pinchas Winston. "Just Desserts," Torah.org, 1995-2007, http://www.torah.org/learning/perceptions/5761/bamidbar.html.

83. 'Spread, Spot, Stay, Send' is my summary of Jesus' mission strategy displayed in Luke 10:1-12 and Acts 16:13-15.

84. I write more about this in *Talmadim*, another book in this series (publication pending as of this writing).

85. James 4:2.

86. Actual quote is by John Wimber in *Power Evangelism* (Ventura, CA: Regal Books, 2009), 35: "*Once we place our trust in Christ, we are drafted into a fierce spiritual battle. Often, Kingdom life is likened to a Caribbean cruise on a luxury liner. People change into their leisure clothes, grab their suntan lotion, and saunter down to the docks. What a shock it is when they find that living in the Kingdom is really more like enlisting in the navy and doing battle with a vicious enemy.*"

JOIN OUR

HAVERIM™
DEVOTIONS
FACEBOOK GROUP

FACEBOOK.COM/GROUPS/HD

All over the world people are being empowered by the Bible to learn how to think, not just what to think.

SHARE IDEAS
DAILY
TALK TO OTHERS
DISCOVER TOGETHER
CREATIVE STUDY

JOIN OUR ANNUAL
FACEBOOK
MONTH LONG
EVENT
GLOBAL HD

POWERED BY THE PAIS MOVEMENT
INTENDED I IMPLIED I INTERPRETED I INSPIRED

Instilling the Pais distinctive approach to study.

UNIQUE INTERACTION
Haverim Devotions™ offers four different ways to interact with the same passage of scripture. It is a new type of Bible Study that connects ancient methods with the emerging values of *Experience, Participation, Imagination, & Connection*.

WHY?
DISCOVER
THE HEART
OF GOD

HOW?
BEYOND
CURRICULUM
TO CULTURE

UNIQUE COMMUNITY
Haverim Devotions™ is simple but not shallow. Instead of a pre-set curriculum, it teaches students *how* to think rather than *what* to think. It is therefore more inclusive and transferable to those connected with God as well as those leaning towards Him.

UNIQUE STUDY
Haverim Devotions™ offers the community a study that asks a simple question: *What is in the heart of God?* It trains participants to approach and apply scripture through the *Intended, Implied, Interpreted, & Inspired* meanings.

WHAT?
4 LEVELS
1 PURPOSE

"This is not a list of steps to execute but an invitation to come and experience. This is not a presentation tool but a participation tool. This is not a matter of providing the right answers but provoking the right questions. This is not an opportunity to consume knowledge but to connect with others to share it."
Paul Gibbs
Haverim Devotions™ Creator

For more information about Haverim Devotions™ please contact us at info@paismovement.com or check out

WWW.HAVERIMDEVOTIONS.COM

About the Author

Paul Gibbs is the founder and global director of Pais. He and his wife Lynn have two sons, Joel and Levi. Originally from Manchester, England, the Gibbs family moved to the USA in 2005 to globally expand Paul's vision of "missionaries making missionaries."

Paul began pioneering openings into Manchester schools as an associate minister in 1987. In September 1992, he founded the Pais Project, initially a one-team gap year project in north Manchester, which has exploded globally, training and placing thousands of missionaries and reaching millions of students throughout Europe, North and South America, Asia, and Africa. Since then, Paul has developed two other branches of Pais: one that equips churches in missional strategies and one that provides businesses with cause marketing strategies. Under Paul's leadership, the Pais Movement continues to grow, launching initiatives and resources to further God's Kingdom.

Paul gained national recognition in the UK for mentoring and training leaders. He has written three books and speaks throughout the world at venues, which include Bible colleges and seminaries, churches, leadership retreats, and youth conferences. His primary topics are pioneering, leadership development, the Kingdom of God, and ancient practices for post-modern times.

Paul enjoys swimming, surfing, skiing, sailing, snowboarding, and is an avid Manchester United fan!

www.paulgibbs.info
www.facebook.com/paulcgibbs
www.twitter.com/paulcgibbs

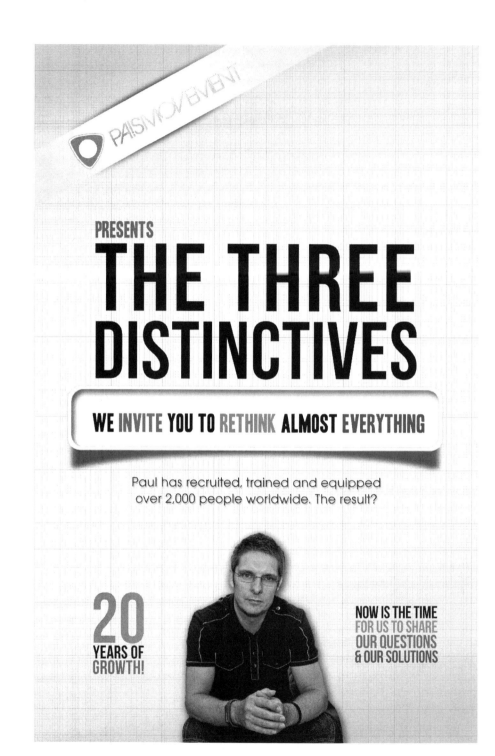

INTRODUCING PAUL GIBBS

non-profit ceo | pioneer | author | mentor

Making our primary concern to advance the Kingdom of God in our world.

BEYOND ATTRACTION TO APPLICATION

Equipping the saints to realize the mission they've been called to!

Vision - Where does it really come from?

Creativity - What is the missing ingredient?

Faith - How does it grow?

Strategy - Is there a divine way of reaching my world?

WHY?
TO SPARK A
GLOBAL
MOVEMENT

HOW?
AN ALTERNATIVE
APPROACH

BEYOND EDUCATION TO EXPERIENCE

Equipping the saints to understand the practices they've been called to!

Experiential - Are there invitations that can be experienced?

Participatory - Is there an opportunity that everyone can participate in?

Imaginal - What are the images that provoke the best questions?

Connected - How can an idea flow purely through a community?

BEYOND CURRICULUM TO CULTURE

Equipping the saints to participate in the conversation they've been called to!

Intended - How does context help us understand the simple message?

Implied - How do connections help us discover the hinted message?

Interpreted - How does collaboration help us search for the message?

Inspired - How does contemplation help us uncover the secret message?

WHAT?
MISSION
DISCIPLESHIP
STUDY

For twenty years Paul has recruited and taught over 2,000 apprentices to give their lives away to a higher calling. To leave all that is familiar, in order to change the world. To do it full time and without a salary. So it makes sense that so many church and organizational leaders are intrigued. It explains why they are asking questions of Paul. After the successful integration of the Pais 3 distinctives outside of Pais, it has become clear to us that we have something special to offer. Our understanding of what encourages people to live above the line, what motivates them to go beyond their job description, can transform a group of individuals into a purpose driven team of collaborators.

For more information about Paul and what we can offer:

WWW.PAISMOVEMENT.COM

133

Other Books by Paul Clayton Gibbs

The Kingdom Trilogy

The Line and the Dot

The first in the trilogy, this book studies Kingdom pioneering. Using the motif of a pioneer, it presents an alternative view of vision in the Kingdom of God.

The Cloud and the Line

The second in the trilogy, this book examines Kingdom principles. Using the motif of a knight, it presents an alternative view of religion in the Kingdom of God.

The Seed and the Cloud

The third in the trilogy, this book analyzes Kingdom patterns. Using the motif of a pilgrim, it presents an alternative view of guidance in the Kingdom of God.

www.facebook.com/thelineandthedot
www.facebook.com/thecloudandtheline
www.facebook.com/theseedandthecloud

Available for purchase at www.paismovement.com/resources.

SPARKING A GLOBAL MOVEMENT

ENGLAND I IRELAND I DEUTSCHLAND I USA I CANADA I GHANA I BRASIL I INDIA & MANY MORE

Re-thinking our mission strategies, discipleship programs, and study groups.

THE 3 DISTINCTIVES OF PAIS

Pais exists to spark a Global movement where the Saints' primary concern is to advance the Kingdom of God in their world. The organization does this by equipping them in three distinctive approaches to Mission, Discipleship and Study, using unique programs and training to accomplish this.

WHY?
A UNIQUE APPROACH

HOW?
EMPLOYING THE DISTINCTIVES IN A VARIETY OF COMMUNITIES

THE 3 ELEMENTS OF PAIS

Pais serves the church in three areas. The Pais Project works with young people, bridging the gap between schools and churches. The Pais Collective targets adults and university students by equipping, training, mentoring and resourcing churches. The Pais Venture empowers business leaders to use their organizations in effectively advancing the Kingdom of God in the marketplace.

THE VARIOUS RESOURCES

In these three elements of the youth, adult, and business communities, Pais offers unique programs, training, coaching, and apprentices who act as a catalyst in our three distinctives of mission, discipleship, and study. Pais does not act independently but instead is fully committed to work in partnership. We see ourselves as one 'piece of the pie.'

WHAT?
JOIN THE MOVEMENT OR ADOPT THE MISSION

"Do we need to re-think our mission strategies? For instance, are we really equipping the saints for works of service or simply encouraging the saints to populate our meetings? Is the Kingdom being advanced or merely maintained? At Pais, we have come to the conclusion that we do not need a new kind of program but a new kind of person but what does that look like?"
Paul Gibbs

For more information about Pais and what we can offer please contact us at info@paisproject.com or check out

WWW.PAISMOVEMENT.COM

About the Pais Movement

Our Aim

Pais exists to spark a global movement, where the primary concern of God's people is His Kingdom, and where they are equipped to advance it in their world. We do this through distinctive approaches to mission, discipleship, and study in the areas of youth and schools, churches, and business.

Our Passion

Pais is the New Testament Greek word for 'child' or 'child servant to the king.' Our motto is 'missionaries making missionaries.' We are passionate about the people of our world and are desperate to see them in the relationship with God that He intended us to have. We come alongside schools, churches, and businesses in their endeavor to empower people to grow in their understanding and experience of God.

Our Vision

Mission lies at the heart of Pais. We seek to help both the apprentices and those they touch develop missionary hearts, missionary skills, and missionary lives. As each missionary makes a missionary, we see our world change.

www.paisproject.com
www.facebook.com/paisproject
www.twitter.com/paisproject

PRESENTS

THE FREE
APPRENTICESHIP

INCLUDES FOOD, TRAINING & ACCOMMODATION!

Do you want to train in new forms of Youth Ministry or Church Leadership?
Are you keen to discover a fresh perspective on Mission, Discipleship and Study?

5 CONTINENTS
N.AMERICA
EUROPE
AFRICA ASIA
S.AMERICA

LEADERSHIP
COMMUNICATION
MISSION
TEACH STUDY
DISCIPLESHIP

THE APPRENTICESHIPS AT A GLANCE

ENGLAND I IRELAND I DEUTSCHLAND I USA I CANADA I GHANA I BRASIL I INDIA & MANY MORE

Instilling the Pais distinctives of Mission, Discipleship and Study.

WHAT YOU RECEIVE ON PAIS

The Apprenticeship offers on-the-job training & includes 200+ hours of specialist seminary-style teaching. After three weeks of foundational training, you move into the hands-on phase. There are bi-weekly mentoring sessions, 'Livewire' interactive training videos and teams are brought back together for specific conferences during the year.

WHY?
A UNIQUE AND SPECIAL MISSION

HOW?
TRAIN IN MISSION DISCIPESHIP & STUDY

WHAT YOU GIVE ON PAIS

A Pais Apprenticeship empowers you to do ministry differently. You will be given leadership opportunities in either youth ministry or church leadership. You will learn and teach Pais' three unique distinctives of Mission, Discipleship, and Study. You will use our training but have the space to use your specific gifts and display your unique passions.

THE VARIOUS OPTIONS

There are different lengths of apprenticeships, from our standard 11-month option to our 18-month course; this partly depends on when you want to start and in which nation you want to serve. Many of our apprentices go on to lead teams or serve in other capacities. Our THR33 program offers a long-term opportunity with Pais. At the end of THR33 we will proactively work with you to find a paid position with Pais or a partner church.

WHAT?
11 MONTHS
18 MONTHS
3 YEARS

TAKE THE **PERSONALITY** TEST

Take our quick online test to find out how the Pais apprenticeship will best suit you. It'll just take a few minutes to fill out but will show you the kinds of strengths you will bring to a team, and also what areas you will have the opportunity to excel in.

For more information about Pais and what we can offer please contact us at info@paismovement.com or check out

WWW.PAISMOVEMENT.COM

PRESENTS

PAIS LIFE MENTORS

COACHING YOUNG PEOPLE FOR LIFE!

Come join a movement that is using Haverim Devotions™
around the world to mentor people and expand God's Kingdom.

HOPE
PURPOSE
CONFIDENCE
SERVICE
SELF-DISCOVERY

5 CONTINENTS
N.AMERICA
EUROPE
AFRICA ASIA
S.AMERICA

Printed in Great Britain
by Amazon